TRADITIONAL CHINESE ARTS AND CULTURE

The Great Wall of China in History and Legend

Luo Zhewen and Zhao Luo

FOREIGN LANGUAGES PRESS   BEIJING 1986

First Edition   1986

Translated by
Zeng Xianwu and Wang Zengfen

ISBN 0-8351-1454-6

Copyright 1986 by Foreign Languages Press

Published by Foreign Languages Press
24 Baiwanzhuang Road, Beijing, China

Printed by Foreign Languages Printing House
19 West Chegongzhuang Road, Beijing, China

Distributed by China International Book Trading Corporation (Guoji Shudian),
P.O. Box 399, Beijing, China

Printed in the People's Republic of China

Contents

Preface

To most foreigners the words "the Great Wall" and "China" are nearly synonymous, for their geography textbooks have all taught them about one of the great wonders of the world. For the Chinese it's somewhat the same, for a Chinese saying goes: "You won't be considered a great man if you have not been to the Great Wall."

Just how great is the Great Wall? To explain, some people may tell you it was the only man-made object on earth seen by the astronauts from the moon; others, interested in statistics, may say if you took all the bricks used in the Great Wall and built a wall 5 metres high and 1 metre thick, it would go around the earth once or even more. Or, if the Great Wall was moved to the United States, it would stretch from Philadelphia to Kansas; if it was drawn on a map of Europe, it would equal the distance from Lisbon to Naples. Still others calculate that the labour involved in building the Great Wall would have built 30 Egyptian pyramids — and so it goes.

The long history of the Great Wall is also much discussed. It is generally considered to have been built in the 3rd century B.C. by the First Emperor of the Qin Dynasty — the ambitious Qin Shi Huang. Many legends about him have been passed down to today. During the past 22 centuries people have never ceased to talk about his merits and demerits — a discussion not entirely irrelevant to the Great Wall.

In fact, the Great Wall we see today was not built by Qin Shi Huang but has existed for only 600 years. Strictly speaking, "the Great Wall" should be plural. The first Great Wall of China was built in the 7th century B.C. After that several dozen Great Walls were built by succeeding dynasties. In today's Shandong Province we can still see the remains of the state of Qi's Great Wall built in 555 B.C. If we put together all the great walls built by various dynasties, their total length would be more than 50,000 kilometres, the section in Inner Mongolia alone extending 15,000 kilometres.

As witness to Chinese history during the past 20-odd centuries, the Great Wall enjoyed its golden age during the height of feudal society and gradually lost its functions as feudal society declined. It played a significant role in protecting China from the harassments of the nomadic tribes in the north, ensuring the safety and stability of people's lives in the Central Plain areas. At the same time it was a positive element in encouraging migration, developing frontier areas, and ensuring smooth passage along the Silk Road — the most important link between China and the West.

People in China regard the Great Wall as a symbol of their indestructible national spirit. Since the Opium War in 1840 the Chinese people had fought for freedom and independence. In the 1930s, when the country was suffering from the invasion of the Japanese militarists, the people sang out, "Arise, you who refuse to be slaves! With our flesh and blood, let us build our new Great Wall!" (*March of the Volunteers*) After eight years of bitter struggle they succeeded in driving the invaders out of the country. In 1949 the Chinese at last ended 100 years of foreign aggression and oppression. They stood up, like the Great Wall, in the East of the world.

For hundreds of years poets have praised the Great Wall from the depths of their hearts. A Tang Dynasty poet, Wang Chang-ling, praised its imposing look with the following lines: "Thousands of ranges screening Yumen (Jade Gate)/And in south and north rise peaks." Another Tang Dynasty poet, Wang Zhihuan, vividly described the steepness of the Great Wall: "The Yellow River rises, merging into white clouds/ And one solitary wall is surrounded by peaks thousands of metres high." A scholar in the Song Dynasty named Han Qi praised the dangerous and crucial position of a Great Wall pass: "Among ranges stretching east and west/The defile can allow only a few mounted soldiers to pass." Marshal Chen Yi, the late Vice-Premier, wrote in a *ci* (an ancient poetic form) titled "The Great Wall," "The sky looks lower when you stand on top of Badaling/And the mountain peaks look smaller with the meandering Great Wall reigning over them."

Today, the Great Wall has lost its military function, but it has become a tourist attraction for people from all over the world. The famous passes, such as Shanhaiguan in Hebei Province, Jiayuguan in Gansu Province and Juyongguan, 50 or so kilometres north of Beijing, and a part of the Great Wall on Badaling about 70 kilometres north of Beijing, receive visitors all year round. Photographers shoot their favourite pictures there; artists capture their impressions with paint and brush; but most people simply stand on the wall, awed by its splendour, the surrounding scenery and the sense of history relived.

The Chinese government has paid great attention to the protection and study of the Great Wall. Shanhaiguan, Jiayuguan and the section of the wall on Badaling have been designated major historical relics under state protection. In 1980 the Chinese government held a conference in Hohhot, Inner Mongolia, at which scholars presented several dozen papers on the Great Wall and put forth a number of important suggestions for its protection. Local governments along the Great Wall have taken the part of the wall within their jurisdiction under protection, sending out patrols and explaining to people the wall's significance and their duty to take care of it, for the Great Wall belongs not only to China but to the world.

A Brief History of the Great Wall

The Great Wall first appeared in the 7th century B.C. and was strengthened or expanded in the succeeding 2,300 years virtually by every dynasty. Although a considerable part of the wall built by the various dynasties no longer exists, we can still gather a rough idea of its history from remains discovered in different parts of China and from historical records.

The Great Wall in the Spring and Autumn and Warring States Periods

From the 8th century to the 3rd century B.C. China was divided into many warring princely states headed by enfeoffed princes, who built fortifications around their states — beacon towers and blockhouses gradually connected by walls. They spread over the vast areas near the Huanghe (Yellow River) and the Changjiang (Yangtze River). The short walls were over 100 li* and the longest ones reached 1,000 li.

The Great Wall of Chu The state of Chu in the middle reaches of the Yangtze River was the first to build the Great Wall. According to *Zuo Qiuming's Commentary on the "Spring and Autumn Annals,"* in 656 B.C. Prince Cheng Wang of the state of Chu built a long wall called Fang Cheng to ward off invasions from the state of Qi. The *Commentary on the "Waterways Classic,"* written by Li Daoyuan in the 5th century and based on the investigations of geographers, gives a more detailed description of the direction, location and length of the wall in the north of the state of Chu and also calls it the Great Wall. The Chu wall was nearly 1,000 li long. It started in what is now northwestern Zhushan County in Hubei Province, went north through southeastern Shaanxi and southwestern Henan, and terminated at Miyang County. On the whole, it was shaped like a half circle.

*In modern times, one li equals half a kilometre, but in ancient times it varied from dynasty to dynasty. In the Warring States Period, for instance, one li was equivalent to 346 metres. For details, see "Units of Measure of Each Dynasty" in this book.

— 1 —

Archaeologists have discovered a part of the wall of the state of Chu in Xunyang County, Shaanxi Province. Built of solid rocks, it stretches over 100 kilometres. Some of its gates are still clearly distinguishable.

The Chu wall played an important role in Chinese history. In 624 B.C. the neighbouring state of Jin to the north sent troops to attack the state of Chu. The wall stopped them and they had to retreat. To the west of Chu the wall warded off possible attacks from the strong state of Qin.

The wall of Chu set the pattern for succeeding generations of walls. It was composed of a series of small fortresses, with, between them, walls where the ground was flat and no walls where there were natural barriers of mountains and rivers. Building materials depended on the locality. The wall was generally made of rammed earth; where there was no earth to be found, of rock.

The Great Wall of Qi The state of Qi, whose domain was within the borders of present-day Shandong Province, had already started its wall by the 5th century B.C. It stretched 1,000 li from today's Pingyin County in the west to Jiaoxian County, ending at the sea. It was meant mainly to guard against invasions from the state of Chu in the south.

Today, remains of the wall of the state of Qi can be found in Laiwu and Tai'an counties in Shandong Province. We can see from these that the wall was usually

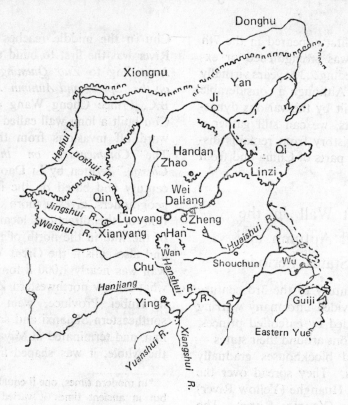

SKETCH MAP OF THE GREAT WALL OF THE WARRING STATES PERIOD

The Great Wall.

The Great Wall as seen through a gateway.

Charming autumn at the Great Wall.

Summer at the Great Wall.

The Great Wall in the vicinity of Juyongguan, located at Badaling 60 kilometres northwest of Beijing, was the gateway to protect Beijing. Walls were built here during the Ming Dynasty (1368-1644).

Section of a mural in a Han Dynasty tomb at Horinger, Inner Mongolia, showing the arched gateway at Juyongguan.

Juyongguan.

Cloud Terrace at Juyongguan, built in the Yuan Dynasty (1271-1368). The arched gateway has vivid carvings.

The Buddhist *Dharani Sutra*, written in Sanskrit, Tibetan, Mongolian, Uygur, Han and Xixia, covers the gateway's walls.

A watchtower on the Great Wall.

Summer visitors at Badaling.

Huangcaoliang Great Wall in Mentougou on the western outskirts of Beijing. It was built by General Qi Jiguang and his soldiers in the Ming Dynasty.

Built over precipitous mountains, the wall exemplified a magnificent boldness of vision; when the slopes are luxuriantly green, the scenery is beautiful.

The wall is crenelated on both sides — a distinctive feature.

Gubeikou and Jinshanling Great Wall   Gubeikou, located on
the boundary between Beijing and Luanping County, Hebei
Province, was a strategic pass from Beijing to northern Hebei.
Built in the Ming Dynasty, the pass, along with the Great Wall,
was an important line of defence for Beijing.

Jinshanling Great Wall. The square structure is a watchtower.

Gubeikou Great Wall.

Barrier walls are special structures on Jinshanling Great Wall. If enemy forces stormed up the fortification, defenders could make use of the barriers, step by step, to resist.

This watchtower, built 400 years ago, was used for housing troops and storing grain. It is now dilapidated.

Walls enclosing the watchtower.

Honeycomblike castles on the mountainside.

The east gatetower.

Shanhaiguan, between the Yanshan Mountains on the west and Bohai Sea on the east, is strategically important. It is known as the First Pass Under Heaven.

Outer wall of the east gate. The moat is 17 metres wide and 7 metres deep.

The Ninghai ruins, where the Great Wall meets Bohai.

Meng Jiangnu Temple, 6.5 kilometres northeast of Shanhaiguan. It was built in memory of Meng Jiangnu, whose tears, according to legend, brought down the Great Wall.

Statue of Meng Jiangnu.

Bianjinlou Gatetower is situated in Daixian County, Shanxi Province. The "Three Passes" written on the horizontal board refers to Yanmenguan, Ningwuguan and Piantouguan.

Yanmenguan, or Wild Goose Pass, located in northern Shanxi Province, was an important station along the ancient Great Wall. It was said the terrain was so steep, it was difficult even for wild geese to fly over.

Statues of Yang Ye and his wife She Taijun in the ancestral hall of the Yang family in Daixian County. Yang Ye was a Great Wall garrison general in the Song Dynasty (960-1279). Jiayuguan, located in Gansu Province, was the western end of the Ming Dynasty Great Wall.

The last brick. The story goes that the builder made precise calculations before constructing Jiayuguan. To prove his accuracy he ordered one extra brick. At the end of construction one brick remained. It is displayed inside the western gatetower.

A magnificent view of the western gatetower.

The Han Dynasty Great Wall near Hohhot in Inner Mongolia.

Remains of the Han Great Wall near Yumenguan in Gansu Province. It was built of reed, tamarisk, sand and rock.

The Qin Great Wall in Lintao County, Gansu Province.

Zhenbeitai, an important defence post for the Ming Great Wall in Yulin, Shaanxi Province.

The Ming Great Wall in Yongchang County, Gansu Province.

The Great Wall on the bank of the Yellow River near Pianguan in Shanxi Province.

A defence post in the Great Wall on the bank of the Yellow River in Fugu County, Shaanxi Province.

The Great Wall was built by taking advantage of the natural terrain. This watchtower was built out of a mountain at Beizhen in Liaoyang City, Liaoning Province.

The **Great Wall** used local materials wherever possible. These walls were built of rocks and the watchtower was built of bricks.

made of loess on flat land and of rock in mountainous areas. The remaining sections are 4 to 5 metres thick and 1 to 4 metres high, depending on the amount of destruction.

The Great Wall of Zhongshan Zhongshan was a small state in the middle of today's Hebei Province. To prevent attacks from the strong neighbouring states of Zhao and Jin to the southwest, in 369 B.C. it built a wall of more than 500 li along the Taihang Mountains on the border between Hebei and Shanxi provinces. Nevertheless, Zhongshan was conquered by the state of Zhao in 296 B.C.

The Great Wall of Wei Situated in today's Henan and Shaanxi provinces, Wei was the strongest principality at the beginning of the Warring States Period. It built two walls as protection against the state of Qin in the west and Quanrong in the northwest. One wall, built between 361 and 351 B.C., was called Hexi Changcheng (Great Wall West of the River). It started at Huashan Mountain and followed the Yellow River's west bank northward, stretching over 1,000 li. Remains of the wall can still be seen in Huayin, Hancheng, Yan'an, Suide and other places in Shaanxi Province. The other wall, in Henan Province, was built in 355 B.C. Its south end was near Zhengzhou; its north end west of Yuanyang, a total length of about 600 li.

The Great Wall of Qin The state of Qin, situated in today's Shaanxi and Gansu provinces, was trying to expand eastward and unite China; therefore there was no need for it to build walls between Qin and its neighbouring states to the east. However, to its northwest were the strong Xiongnu (Huns). As the Xiongnu constantly went southward to harass neighbouring states, they posed a great threat to Qin. Therefore the state of Qin began building a wall in 324 B.C. to guard against invasions by the Xiongnu. This wall stretched about 2,000

li, starting in Minxian County in Gansu Province, going northward to Lanzhou, turning east and reaching the Yellow River in the northeast corner of Shaanxi Province.

The Great Wall of Yan The state of Yan, in ancient times a big state in northeastern China, built walls along its northern and southern borders. The wall in the south was called the Great Wall of Yishui, because most of it followed the Yishui River. Its total length was about 500 li, starting in Yixian County in Hebei Province, going southeastward past Xushui and Renqiu and reaching the vicinity of Wen'an County. It was built around the beginning of the 4th century B.C. to prevent the invasion of Yan by Zhao, backed up by the state of Qin.

Yan's northern wall was the last one built during the Spring and Autumn and Warring States periods. It was also the longest one, stretching over 2,400 li. Built in about 254 B.C. to prevent harassments from the Donghu people in the east, the wall started in the vicinity of today's Zhangjiakou in Hebei Province, went northeast through Inner Mongolia, entered Liaoning Province and finally reached Liaoyang. Remains of the wall can still be found in these places.

The Great Wall of Zhao The state of Zhao, situated in today's Hebei and Henan provinces, also built two walls. One of them, called Zhangfu Great Wall, was constructed in 333 B.C. along Zhao's southern border. It ran for more than 400 li along the northern bank of the Zhangshui River as protection against the states of Wei and Qin. Its remains can still be found in the vicinity of Linzhang and Cixian counties in Hebei Province.

Zhao's northern wall was built in 312 B.C. by Prince Wu Ling, a monarch daring in his reforms and promotion of cultural exchanges among the various nationalities. The wall was part of his defence against invasions of the Hu people. It started at today's Xuanhua in Hebei, went west towards the borders of Inner Mongolia, and reached Gaoque (situated north of the Yellow River in Inner Mongolia), a distance of about 1,300 li. Remains of the wall still meander through the Daqing, Wula and Langshan mountains.

Thus, as various princes in the Spring and Autumn and Warring States periods tried to annex one another's territories and gain dominance, they built walls to defend themselves and attack others. These walls, except for a small part used as the basis of the Great Wall erected by the First Emperor of Qin, had all been destroyed. Yet even these few remains are of great significance in the study of the history of the Great Wall and the political and military situation in that society.

The Great Wall of Qin Shi Huang's Times

The Great Wall began to be called Ten Thousand Li Great Wall in the time of Qin Shi Huang. Therefore, people always associate the Great Wall with Qin Shi Huang.

He was an outstanding statesman at the beginning of Chinese feudal society. In 221 B.C. he ended the long period of division and separatist rule and established the first united country in Chinese history. After uniting China, Qin Shi Huang took a series of measures to consolidate the unity, one of which was the building of the Great Wall.

At that time the areas to the north, west and southwest of the Qin Empire were inhabited by minority nationalities who had just entered or were entering the stage of slave society. Among these, the Xiongnu in the north and the Donghu in the northeast constituted the biggest threat. Therefore, after uniting China, internally Qin Shi Huang continued to crack down on the remnant forces of the nobles of the conquered states while externally he sent troops north

to resist the Xiongnu and built the Great Wall to strengthen the frontier defence, thus preserving the state's relatively advanced agricultural production and protecting people's lives. Also, according to the "Biography of Meng Tian" in *Records of the Historian* by Sima Qian, "Having united China, Qin Shi Huang appointed General Meng Tian as the head of 300,000 soldiers

Qin Shi Huang

to go north to drive the Rong and Di out and recover the areas south of the Yellow River Bend, and to build the Great Wall, using the steep and difficult terrain to guard the passes. The Great Wall started at Lintao and ended at Liaodong, stretching over 10,000 li." Meng Tian's drive to the north took place in 215 B.C. He recovered the Xiongnu-occupied areas in the Yellow River Bend, then he continued to lead his troops north across the Yellow River and recovered vast areas north of the Bend. He also erected fortifications along the Yellow River and the Yinshan Mountains and built the northern part of the Ten Thousand Li Great Wall. The western part started at Lintao; it was rebuilt from

— 4 —

a wall erected by the state of Qin during the Warring States Period. Its eastern part, incorporating the old walls of the states of Zhao and Yan, stretched between Gaoque in the west and Liaodong in the east. Begun in 217 B.C., the Ten Thousand Li Great Wall was completed in 210 B.C.

To consolidate his country, Qin Shi Huang not only built new walls but tore down old ones. After the unification of China, he gave orders to demolish all the old walls and passes built by the various princely states. This event is recorded on a stone tablet at Qinhuangdao marking Qin Shi Huang's eastern tour of inspection. It says: "After I overpowered all the princes, China for the first time enjoyed peace. I have taken down all the old walls and passes and leveled the steep landscapes. Now the common people are pacified and no longer have any fear of war. Men work on the land, while women are likewise engaged in their work."

General Meng Tian

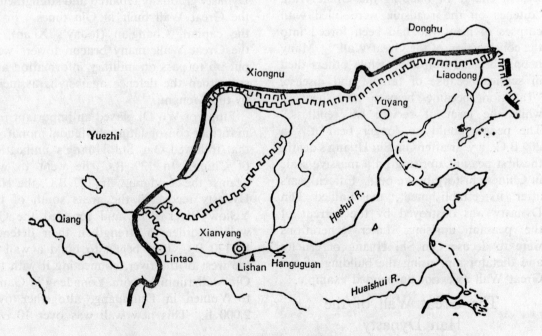

SKETCH MAP OF THE QIN DYNASTY GREAT WALL

— 5 —

By tearing down all the walls, passes and fortifications built by the various states as protection against each other, Qin Shi Huang had eliminated the conditions by which the nobles of those states maintained their separate rules.

After completion of the Great Wall, "the Xiongnu went north for fear of Qin." They did not dare let their horses graze on southern pastures for more than 10 years. This shows that the Great Wall was significant in consolidating the unification of China and protecting the security of the Qin Empire.

Yet the building of the Great Wall and other large construction projects forced many people to work under hard conditions, with severe punishment, taking many working people out of productive activities. People's dissatisfaction rose with each passing day. According to Huai Nan Zi's "Principles of the World" in *The Book of the Prince of Huainan*, when Meng Tian was in charge of building the Great Wall, "ditches on the roadside were filled with corpses of men who had been forced into the construction of the Great Wall." Many people became homeless, while others died in service because of fatigue and disease. "Taxation became heavier and heavier, while the term of service was endless." The people could no longer bear it. In 209 B.C., a year after Qin Shi Huang's death, the first peasant uprising on a massive scale in Chinese history broke out. Fifteen years after its establishment, the unified Qin Dynasty was destroyed by the torrent of the peasant uprising. Later generations were to accuse Qin Shi Huang of cruelty and dictatorship, using the building of the Great Wall as a not unfounded example.

The Great Wall of the Han Dynasty

Extensive as the Ten Thousand Li Great Wall of Qin Shi Huang was, the Great Wall of the Han Dynasty was even larger, for walls were built outside the original ones. The total length of the Han Great Wall was over 20,000 li, the section between Dunhuang and Liaodong covering 11,500 li. So the Han Dynasty's wall was the longest in the history of China.

The Great Wall of Han was primarily built to guard against the Xiongnu. In the first years of the Western Han Dynasty (towards the end of the 3rd century B.C.), under the rule of Mao Dun, the Xiongnu became more and more powerful and continually went south to invade and occupy the land of the Han. Having just been established, the Han Dynasty could not afford to send a lot of troops to fight the Xiongnu, so they adopted a conciliationist policy. They married daughters of the royal house to chieftains of the Xiongnu in exchange for momentary peace, but the Xiongnu did not stop their harassments. Therefore, starting in 158 B.C., the Han Dynasty gradually repaired and strengthened the Great Wall built in Qin times. From the capital, Chang'an (today's Xi'an), to the Great Wall, many beacon towers were put up to pass on military information and strengthen the defence against harassments by the Xiongnu.

Emperor Wu Di played an important role in further consolidating the feudal monarchy that followed Qin Shi Huang's unification of China. In 129 B.C. he went to war against the Xiongnu. In 127 B.C. the Han Dynasty recovered the areas south of the Yellow River Bend and repaired the Qin wall in order to strengthen their defence. In 120 B.C. they began to build a wall to the west of the river, connecting it with the Qin wall running from Yongdeng in Gansu to Yumen in Dunhuang, altogether over 2,000 li. This new wall was over 10 *chi**

*One *chi* in the Han period was equivalent to 0.23 metre.

high and more than 3 *chi* wide and extremely solid. Every 5 to 10 li soldiers were stationed on beacon towers to look out for the enemy. If any were sighted, they lit weeds they had gathered as a signal. Many small castles, called *zhang*, were also equip-

Emperor Wu Di

ped with fire signals, and many soldiers were stationed in them. By 101 B.C. the building of such fortifications had reached the western rim of the Salt Marsh (modern Lop Nur in Xinjiang).

Emperor Wu Di further developed and improved the design of the Great Wall. Alongside the wall and inside and outside it at certain distances from it, many defensive structures, called *lie cheng* (castles in a row) or *ting zhang* (obstacles), were built with an eye to the shape of the landscape. Beacon towers connected them, forming a more complete defensive complex. To strengthen contact between the capital and various localities, many other beacon towers and obstacles were built from the capital to all the important areas of the country. This defensive project helped consolidate the position of the Han Dynasty, guaranteeing the security of people's lives. After this, the Xiongnu fled to far-off places.

Remains of the Han Great Wall, obstacles, beacon towers and castles can still be seen in today's Xinjiang, Gansu, Ningxia, Inner Mongolia, Shanxi and Hebei provinces.

The policy begun in the Qin Dynasty of sending garrison troops or peasants to open up wasteland and grow food grains was important in developing production and actively preparing for or against war. It was also closely connected with the building of the Great Wall. The Han Dynasty inherited the policy, encouraging people to live in the frontier areas, open up the land,

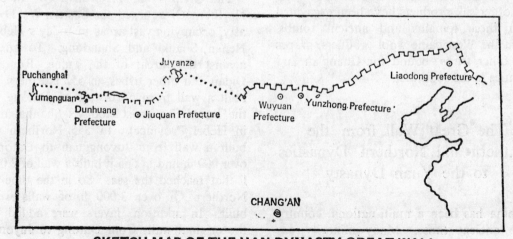

SKETCH MAP OF THE HAN DYNASTY GREAT WALL

build water conservancy works and plough the earth in order to bolster a wartime economy. The policy was effective in fortifying the frontier defence, developing the border regions and boosting frontier economy and culture.

The wall west of the Yellow River, built in the Western Han Dynasty, was also of great significance in opening up East-West transportation and developing China's economic and cultural exchanges with European and other Asian countries. Two thousand years ago Chinese silk fabrics were transported along the Silk Road, passing through Sogdiana, Parthia and Syria, to reach countries in the Mediterranean region, where they enjoyed a high reputation. From Chang'an the road covered 20,000 li, with more than half under the control of the Han Dynasty. At that time it was divided into southern and northern routes. The southern route started at Dunhuang, went along the rim of the Tarim Basin and reached Kashi. The northern route also started at Dunhuang but went west, crossing the desert along the southern rim of the Tianshan Mountains and meeting the southern road at Kashi. Along this ancient road there are still remains of the Han Great Wall, obstacles, castles and beacon towers. Many seals, books made of silk or wooden slats and other silk products have been excavated from these remains and ancient tombs. From the West came wool products, grapes and other fruits, bound for Chang'an and counties in the southeast.

The Great Wall from the Southern and Northern Dynasties to the Yuan Dynasty

China has been a multi-national country since ancient times. Many minority nationalities were once in control of China, and their rulers, after gaining the economically and culturally advanced areas, built walls to prevent the harassments of other nationalities. From the Southern and Northern Dynasties to the Yuan Dynasty (5th to 14th centuries) almost all the walls were built by minority nationality rulers. The Northern Wei, Northern Qi and Kin dynasties all built walls on a large scale.

The Great Wall of Northern Wei The ruler of the Northern Wei Dynasty was of the Xianbeituoba, originally a nomadic tribe. After dominating the Central Plain areas, where agriculture was the major concern, it developed a feudal social economy, and for a time the country was very strong. However, another strong nomadic tribe, called Rouran, to the north along with the Qidan to the northeast, constantly ventured south to sack the country. So the Northern Wei adopted the measure taken by the Qin and the Han to guard against the Xiongnu. In A.D. 423 a wall was built from Hebei in the east to Wuyuan in Inner Mongolia, a distance of over 2,000 li. In 446 another wall was built from Juyongguan near Beijing to Hequ County in Shanxi Province. This wall was 1,000 li long, half-embracing the southern side of Datong, the capital of the Northern Wei.

The Great Wall of Northern Qi In 550 Northern Qi annexed the Eastern Wei Dynasty, occupying vast areas in today's Hebei, Henan, Shanxi and Shandong. To guard against the threat of the Tujue, Rouran, Qidan and other tribes, in 552 Northern Qi built a wall from northwest of Datong to the Bohai Sea coast (today's Shanhaiguan in Hebei Province). In 555 Northern Qi built a wall from Juyongguan to Datong, over 900 li, and in 565 it built a wall of 2,000 li that reached the sea. So in the time of Northern Qi over 3,000 li of walls were built. In addition, layers were added to the original walls from Datong to Juyongguan.

To guard against the Northern Zhou Dynasty, in 563 Northern Qi also built a wall from Xuanhua in the north to Fuping in the south in Hebei Province.

The Great Wall of Northern Zhou After annexing Western Wei in 557, Northern Zhou occupied Hebei, Shanxi, Shandong and other areas. As precautions against the Tujue and the Qidan in the north, Northern Zhou strengthened the former wall of Western Wei in the north and, in 579, built a wall that stretched from Yanmenguan in Shanxi to Jieshi in Hebei Province.

The Great Wall of Sui In 581 Emperor Wen Di of Sui unified south and north, ending the 400-year rule of separate feudal states. In order to guard against the Tujue, Qidan, Tuguhun and others, he had many times mobilized people to build the Great Wall. In all, the Sui Dynasty worked on the Great Wall seven times, yet most of the time it was only to improve the original walls, not extend them.

During the Tang, Song and Liao dynasties, wall building nearly ceased. The Tang Dynasty overwhelmed the Tujue and extended its boundary as far as the Gobi Desert, making the Great Wall useless. Although the Song Dynasty unified the Central Plain, it was confined to an area south of the walls of the former Qin, Han and the Northern Dynasties, and those walls were within the domains of Liao and Kin. Soon, the Song Dynasty's control retreated to south of the Yangtze River, so rebuilding the Great Wall was out of the question.

The Great Wall of Kin In 1115 the Nüzhen in the northeast established the Kin Dynasty and eliminated the Liao and Song dynasties successively. The Kin Dynasty bordered on Mongolia to the northwest, so it built walls on a massive scale for the purpose of defence. The two walls of the Kin Dynasty were the old and new wall of Mingchang.

The old wall of Mingchang used to be called the Great Wall of Wushu or the border castle of Jinyuan. It was approximately on the bank of today's Heilong River northwest of the Hinggan range in Heilongjiang Province and was over 1,000 li in length.

The new wall of Mingchang, far within the old wall, was also called the Inner Wall of Kin. It started in the Yellow River Bend area and ended at the Songhua River in today's Heilongjiang Province, over 3,000 li.

The Yuan Dynasty's territory extended over Asia to Europe and its border was far away from the northern Great Wall. The rulers themselves were originally nomads north of the Great Wall, so the wall was of little significance to them. Yet they still strengthened many passes of the wall in order to prevent the Han and other nationalities from rising in arms and to check and examine passing merchants.

The Ten Thousand Li Great Wall of the Ming Dynasty

After the conquest of the Yuan Dynasty by the Ming, the Mongolian nobles fled back to their homeland, but they still kept harassing and plundering the people in the south. At the same time the Nüzhen were rising in the northeast. To guard against both Mongolians and Nüzhen, the Ming rulers paid great attention to defence of their northern borders. Throughout the 200 years of their rule, the Ming virtually never stopped building and strengthening the Great Wall. The scale of the project was so vast that, except for the work of Qin Shi Huang and the Han emperor Wu Di, it outstripped that of all other dynasties. Moreover, the technology was improved to a great extent, so the structure was more solid and provided better defence.

In the first year of the Ming Dynasty (1368) the first emperor Zhu Yuanzhang

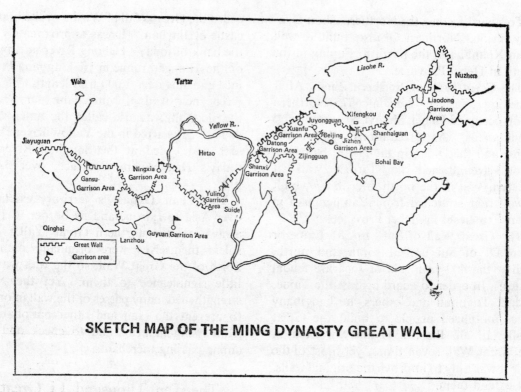

Wala · Tartar · Liaohe R. · Nuzhen · Jiayuguan · Yellow R. · Xifengkou · Liaodong Garrison Area · Juyongguan · Xuanfu Garrison Area · Beijing · Shanhaiguan · Datong Garrison Area · Jizhen Garrison Area · Gansu Garrison Area · Hetao · Zijingguan · Bohai Bay · Ningxia Garrison Area · Shanxi Garrison Area · Yulino Garrison Area · Suide · Qinghai · Guyuan Garrison Area · Lanzhou · Great Wall · Garrison area

SKETCH MAP OF THE MING DYNASTY GREAT WALL

sent General Xu Da to supervise the building of the Great Wall in Juyongguan and other places. In 1381 walls in Shanhaiguan and other locations were built. By the end of the 16th century, when Qi Jiguang was in command of the Jizhou Garrison Area, over 1,000 beacon towers were constructed along the line linking Shanhaiguan and Juyongguan. At crucial points, especially in the vicinity of Juyongguan, Shanhaiguan and Yanmenguan to the north of the then capital Beijing, he built many layers of wall, in some places more than 20 layers, and erected many observation posts and beacon towers. Between 1506 and 1521, over 3,000 beacon towers were built in the vicinity of Xuanfu and Datong. Work on the Great Wall lasted more than 200 years, until 1600, and some castles and passes were still being built towards the end of the Ming Dynasty.

The Ming Great Wall starts at the Yalu River in the east and ends at Jiayuguan in the west, measuring over 12,700 li. Because the part from Shanhaiguan to the Yalu River was rather poorly built, it has sus-

Zhu Yuanzhang

tained more serious damage than other parts. The part from Shanhaiguan to Jiayuguan, relatively solid, is better preserved. It also has two passes in the east and west on both sides. For a long time, therefore, people have thought of the Great Wall as starting in Shanhaiguan and ending in Jiayuguan. It is this section of the Ming wall

They were called the Inner Great Wall and the Outer Great Wall. The inner and outer walls in Hebei, Beijing, Shanxi and Inner Mongolia were the northwestern defensive screen of the Ming capital of Beijing. It was equal in importance to the Great Wall of the Jizhou Garrison Area, between Shanhaiguan and Juyongguan. The inner three

THE MING DYNASTY GREAT WALL AT THE
LOUZIYING—HEQUYING SECTION WEST OF PIANGUAN PASS

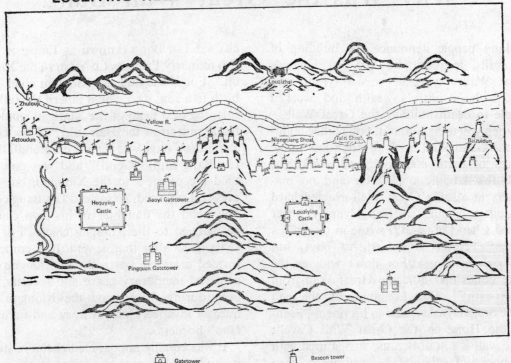

that we see today.

To strengthen the defensive capabilities of the wall and dispatch soldiers along it, the Ming Dynasty improved the passes and divided the wall into nine garrison areas. Every garrison area had a commander in charge of defence and repairs.

With over 1,000 passes, each garrison area controlled a number of them. West of Juyongguan the wall separated into northern and southern lines, which joined together in Laoying near Pianguan in Shanxi.

passes of Juyongguan, Daomaguan and Zijingguan, near Beijing, and the outer three passes of Yanmenguan, Ningwuguan and Piantouguan to the west, were crucial, constituting the essential defence for the Ming capital and southeast areas. They were often manned with a concentration of forces.

Besides the Ten Thousand Li Great Wall in the north, the Ming Dynasty built 380 li of walls in Hunan and Guizhou, stationing soldiers there to guard against aggression from the southwest.

Why Was the Great Wall Built?

Many people denounce the building of the walls, in particular Qin Shi Huang's Great Wall, saying he was a tyrant who wasted the country's wealth and worked people to death building the Great Wall.

When you think about it, you realize building the Great Wall used up countless cubic metres of earth and rock and workdays. With few labourers available and no machinery at all, the Great Wall exacted hard and bitter labour. A Han Dynasty writer named Chen Lin (?-217) wrote in one of his poems: "Never give birth to boys, but feed girls with meat/For don't you see the white bones that hold the Great Wall from underneath?" Wu Longhan, at the end of the Song Dynasty, said in his poem "Feeding the Horse in the Great Wall Cave": "The wall is so tall because it is stuffed with the bones of soldiers/The wall is so deep because it is watered with the soldiers' blood." Another poem depicts the Great Wall thus: "The northern frontier is devoid of human trace/But the crying of ghosts fills the air space."

Were there other ways to achieve peace on the border without building the Great Wall?

Two ways were tried: the tie of marriage and the contribution of property and money.

Was marriage effective? Liu Jing, an advisor at the beginning of the Han Dynasty, advised Liu Bang (known as Emperor Gao Zu) to marry Princess Lu Yuan to the Xiongnu. For if she and the Xiongnu chief gave birth to a son, who would inherit the father's title, the next head of the Xiongnu would be the grandson of the Han ruler. How could a grandson wage war against his grandfather? Liu Bang said, "Good!" and was going to send the princess to the Xiongnu, but Empress Lü objected, so instead Liu Bang could only send the daughter of his own clan to be married to the Xiongnu chief. For 100 years or so after that, several Han emperors formed marriage ties with the Xiongnu and achieved temporary peace and security, but even during this period the Xiongnu frequently invaded Han territory and harassed Han's borders.

It was equally impossible to achieve stability and prevent nomadic tribes in the north and west from invading Han territory by sending them tremendous amounts of property and money. According to "Biographies of Xiongnu Celebrities" in *Records of the Historian*, the Xiongnu "moved about in search for water and grass; they were a nomadic people who had no agriculture.... Men could use bows and were all well versed in horsemanship. When they were better off, they would travel about with their livestock and make their livelihood out of hunting. When they were desperate, they would

Jinshanling Great Wall in Luanping County, Hebei Province.

Chu Great Wall, built of rocks, in southeastern Shaanxi Province.

Wei Great Wall in Hancheng, Shaanxi Province.

Section of Wei Great Wall.

Qin Great Wall in Lintao, Gansu Province.

Qin Shi Huang Great Wall in Hengshan County, Shaanxi Province.

Meng Tian's tomb in Suide County, Shaanxi Province.

Yan and Qin Great Wall in Weichang County, Hebei Province.

Yan Great Wall in Weichang County, Hebei Province.

Zhao Great Wall in Baotou, Inner Mongolia.

Han Great Wall in Hohhot, Inner Mongolia.

Han (left) and Ming (right) beacon towers in Yongchang County, Gansu Province.

Ming (high) and Sui (low) Great Wall in Yanchi County, Ningxia Hui Autonomous Region.

Sandaoguan Great Wall in the Helan Mountains, Ningxia Hui Autonomous Region.

Beacon tower on the bank of the Wuding River in Northern Shaanxi Province.

Ruins of Great Wall on the bank of the Yalu River, Liaoning Province.

make preparations for wars. They would advance when the circumstances were favourable and retreat when they were not, not at all ashamed of running away. They forgot all courtesy and integrity in face of a little interest.... They took their booty for granted and enslaved the captured. So their purpose in fighting was to gain profit."

It is clear from the above account that the Xiongnu knew only how to reap profit from robbery. When the settled peasants had good harvests from which the Xiongnu could reap huge profit, food and even people, they saw their gain would be much greater than limited annual contributions. Therefore, plunder became the major occupation of the Xiongnu to gather wealth. They frequently invaded Han territory.

What, then, was the best way to guard against the Xiongnu? Many statesmen in ancient China made very concise and pointed remarks about this problem.

During the reign of Emperor Wen Di of the Han Dynasty, Chao Cuo (220-154 B.C.) presented a memorial to the emperor on building beacon towers to guard against the Hu (Xiongnu) in which he said: "The Hu people wandered about where there was water and grass, different from the people who settled down in the Central Plain areas and engaged in agricultural production. Nowadays, the Hu people graze their sheep and cattle in several places and hunt around the frontier areas. From the former domain of the state of Yan in the east to Gansu in the west, the whole of north China is frequently plundered and harassed by the Hu people. If Your Majesty do not go to the rescue, the people will despair, but if you send soldiers to save the people, there is still the problem of how many soldiers to send — if too few, they won't be able to defeat the Hu; if too many, troop movements will be slow and the Hu people will run away. So the best way to deal with these nomads is to build high walls and deep moats and station soldiers at the fortresses, to build a long wall, set up passes in easily defended terrains and build castles."

In 487, during the Northern Wei Dynasty, a man named Gao Lu made the following suggestion to Emperor Xiao Wen: "The northern Di tribes are good at fighting in the wilderness but not good at attacking a city wall. If we take advantage of their shortcoming and avoid their strong point, they can't constitute any real threat even if they overwhelm us in number. They may come but can't enter our fortifications. To build a long wall takes a lot of manpower for a short time, but it solves the problem once and for all. It will benefit hundreds of generations to come. We should open a door at a critical pass and build small castles on its sides. We should take advantage of the terrain and put a lot of bowmen there. So when the Di tribesmen come to attack us, we can defeat them with the help of the wall. Since they can't scale the wall and there is nothing for them to take in the wilderness, they will go away when the grass has given out. In this way we can uproot the 'wild grass' and get rid of it forever." (See "Biography of Gao Lu", *History of the Wei Dynasty*.)

Like the former one, this suggestion analysed the wandering and harassing characteristics of the Di tribes and stated that only by building walls could the Han guard against the invaders. What the author means by suggesting opening doors at critical passes and building small castles is the building of passes and castles before the gates where they could store grain and station soldiers; they could also be used as command headquarters.

Wei Huan of the Ming Dynasty specially emphasized that to defend the frontiers the most urgently needed thing was to build walls. "Building passes to guard the country — there is no better way to guard against the barbarians! Then we must make use of the steep terrain and, in addition, use manpower to build walls. As for defence, we can't talk about it without steep terrain, but even when we have steep terrain and passes, we can't defend our territory without soldiers."

We can see from the above that the Qin Dynasty simply adopted the method used long ago by its predecessors — building walls. The times required them for defence. Although the cost was immense, there was no other way to prevent the nomadic tribes from going south to harass and plunder.

During the reign of Qin Shi Huang, most of the Yellow and Yangtze river basins were already at a prosperous stage of feudal society, which depended mainly on agricultural production. Stable management and a long period of cultivation were indispensable for good harvests. But at that time, the Xiongnu, who were still at an early stage of the slave system, often went south to plunder wealth, cattle and even people, constituting a major threat to the production and life of the people in the Central Plain. Therefore, the Great Wall not only protected against the Xiongnu but helped the development of production as well.

During the 15 years of the Qin Dynasty, after Qin Shi Huang conquered the six states, the Xiongnu dared not go south to harass the people, so we can see that building the Great Wall, under the historical circumstances of the time, was an effective way of defending the country.

The mere fact that walls were built in every dynasty from pre-Qin to Ming proves their value.

In an age when swords, spears, knives, axes, bows and arrows were the major weapons, walls served to block cavalry, organize defensive forces and light signals — all effective measures. Particularly, Shanhaiguan and Juyongguan, which were steep passes, and Xifengkou and Gubeikou, surrounded by mountains and cliffs, were built in vital places for, as the saying goes, "if one soldier was stationed there, no troops, no matter how many, could take the pass."

The chapter on the "Biographies of Xiongnu Celebrities" in *History of the Han Dynasty* records that in 78 B.C., over 3,000 Xiongnu cavalrymen invaded Wuyuan (in today's Inner Mongolia). But fire signals and observation from the Great Wall were clear, and rescue troops arrived in time to push back the invaders. Lu Zhi of the Tang Dynasty advised, "Build walls on the borders, guard the vital points, dig moats, station troops, be very cautious and good at scouting." With the help of the Great Wall, its passes, castles and beacon towers, an invading enemy, if few in number, could be stopped; if large in number, could have their retreat route blocked. At the best of times enemies ran the risk of being attacked from front and rear at the same time, unable to rescue any troops. Reviewing history, we can see that it was extremely difficult to take the Great Wall and in particular the vital passes by direct attacks. The wall has truly played an important role in military defence.

But all this does not mean that the people could rest in peace or relax their vigilance once they had the Great Wall. Invaders bypassing the passes and taking the wall or officers in charge of defence turning traitor were not rare in history.

Take Juyongguan for example. From Nankou (South Entrance) to Beikou (North Entrance) ran a narrow path of over 30 li: "Caught between cliffs meanders the narrow path like bowels." It was regarded as the most fortified pass under heaven. But Liao defeated Later Tang, Kin defeated Liao and Yuan defeated Kin all through this narrow path. High walls, steep passes and other obstacles all failed.

In 1211 the first emperor of the Yuan Dynasty, Genghis Khan, with his four sons attacked Kin. They fought their way to Juyongguan. The Kin people had the advantage of the steepness of the pass, and, in addition, they melted iron to pour on the gate in order to close it forever. They buried iron caltrops on the slope in front of the wall for over 100 li. With the well-trained defending troops posted on the wall, the whole thing was complete. Genghis Khan looked at the terrain in front of the pass and sighed in frustration. He had an officer named Ja Bal who reported, "From here north, there is a narrow path in the dark forest that allows only one horse with one man on it. I have gone over that path once. If we send our best cavalrymen there quietly, they will cross the pass overnight.

Genghis Khan asked Ja Bal to guide the troops. They went onto the valley path and after a night of fast riding reached Nankou south of Juyongguan by daybreak. The Yuan troops beat drums, blew trumpets and cheered. The Kin soldiers, hardly awake, were thoroughly defeated. The Yuan soldiers encircled the Kin capital called Middle Capital — present-day Beijing.

After more than 400 years, towards the end of the Ming Dynasty, peasant troops headed by Li Zicheng advanced from Shanxi to the east and reached Huailai, then went south to go through Zijingguan to enter the capital. Having been bypassed, Juyongguan, which would have been very difficult to take, proved useless.

As for defending officers surrendering the battle, one episode at Shanhaiguan is most illustrative. Shanhaiguan has the Yanshan Mountains to its north and Bohai Sea to the south, therefore its terrain is most favourable for defence. In addition, the pass and wall were very solid, and outside the wall a forest of fortifications and beacon towers communicated with each other by fire signal — altogether an impregnable bulwark. In 1644 a general named Wu Sangui of the Ming Dynasty was appointed to guard the pass with a great number of troops. Qing soldiers made violent attacks but failed to take the pass. Then peasant forces led by Li Zicheng went north after occupying Beijing and fought a battle with the troops commanded by Wu Sangui. Wu let the Qing troops into the pass to attack the peasant troops. After taking Shanhaiguan, the Qing troops went all the way into Ming territory, finally replacing the Ming Dynasty.

We should also note that the Great Wall was a product of earlier times as a line of defence, effective only against cavalrymen, knives, spears and bows and arrows. Making use of mountains and rivers to build fortifications "to halt the feet of the cavalry" was advantageous. Yet after gunpowder was invented, in the Tang Dynasty, it was used extensively in military affairs in the Song Dynasty in the very strong "thunder gun," "iron gun" and other weaponry. In the Yuan Dynasty there were guns that could tear openings in the wall where soldiers could enter. So the Great Wall gradually lost its effectiveness. This was already very obvious during the wars towards the end of the Ming Dynasty. In 1640 the Qing prince Jierhalang fought with the Ming troops at Xingshan and Songshan in Jinzhou. The Ming general Hong Chengchou led 130,000 soldiers to the rescue. The Qing troops, led by General Duo Duo, lay ambush and used the big guns introduced from the West, which were very effective. The Qing troops encircled Songshan, and the vice-commander turned traitor. The Qing troops used ladders to climb the walls and entered the city at midnight, capturing General Hong Chengchou. During this battle of Jinzhou, the Qing troops used modern artillery to attack the walls and thus succeeded in gaining the initiative and winning final victory.

Because of this, after the Qing entered

Shanhaiguan, walls were no longer built on a large scale. Emperor Kang Xi wrote a poem on his inspection tour of the East Sea:

> Orders and appointments fell like snow-
> flakes
> For the ten-thousand-li wall to reach the
> sea.
> Though thou hadst exhausted all thy
> subjects,
> The empire could never belong to thee.

Emperor Kang Xi was criticizing Qin Shi Huang for building the Great Wall, saying that though it was a huge project and cost tremendous manpower, it had not saved his empire. Therefore Kang Xi adopted a so-called soft policy in order to win over the Mongolian and Tibetan nobles.

Religion became the tool to rule the ideological world.

Although the Qing Dynasty built the so-called willow fences* in the northeast to limit the activities of the headsmen and in a few places repaired part of the old wall as passes or to suppress the people's rebellion, their functions were totally different from those of the original Great Wall.

---

*The willow fence was built within the borders of present-day Liaoning and Jilin provinces. On an earth embankment one metre wide and one metre high, trees planted there per 1.5 metres were connected with a cord, forming a willow fence. A deep moat was dug outside the fence to strengthen it. At important traffic points border gates were erected and soldiers stationed there. The willow fence was designed to prevent people of various nationalities from going outside the borders to gather ginseng, graze cattle or hunt.

The Functions, Military Layout and Structure of the Great Wall

The major functions of the Great Wall can be summarized in the following three points:

1. Prevent harassing and wrecking in order to maintain the stability of the state and the security of the people. This was the main task of the Great Wall.

2. Open up wasteland and grow food grains, and protect the cultivated land to boost production in the frontier regions. When Qin Shi Huang was building the Great Wall, he also set up 12 prefectures along the wall and sent people to open up the land and carry out agriculture and animal husbandry. The jurisdiction of these prefectures extended to regions outside the Great Wall. Emperor Wu Di of the Han Dynasty (reigned 140 to 87 B.C.) increased the numbers of settlers and garrison troops and developed agriculture and animal husbandry systematically. For instance, the digging of wells and *karez* (underground tunnels) was also introduced from the Central Plain into the Western Regions. This policy of opening up frontier regions was passed down from generation to generation. The Great Wall became the best protection for the spread of production.

3. Protect communications and the safe passage of tradesmen. During the reign of Qin Shi Huang the northern regions were connected with the capital, Xianyang, by wide roads, and the 12 prefectures along the Great Wall were also linked by wide roads. There was a constant flow of traffic and trade. The Great Wall was an important guarantee for the safety of these roads. In the Han Dynasty the famous Silk Road was opened to the Western Regions. The western part of the Great Wall was built along this major line of communication between East and West.

Since the Great Wall was mainly used for defence, its layout and structure should naturally accord with this purpose. The

MAP ON THE RELATIONSHIP BETWEEN

THE "SILK ROAD" AND THE GREAT WALL

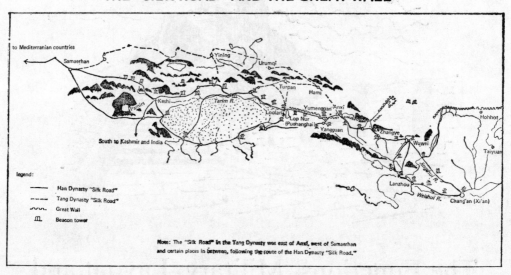

Great Wall appeared like a line 10,000 li long, but actually it was a complete defensive system in itself. It kept extremely close contact with the castles, beacon towers, storehouses, administrative organs of the prefectures and counties, and the capital of the empire, and it was under the direct and unified control of the highest rulers of the various dynasties. Therefore, to understand the structure of the Great Wall, we must first of all have some idea of its military layout. Let's take the defence system of the Ming Dynasty as an example.

The highest organ of military command was the Board of War, in charge of all the defensive tasks in the country. In times of war the President of the Board of War or some other official was appointed by the emperor to be the commanding general. Sometimes the emperor himself would head the army.

The military control areas along the Great Wall were called *zhen* (garrison area). The Ming Dynasty wall had massive defensive strength. From the Yalu River in the east to Jiayuguan in the west it included nine garrison areas altogether. Every garrison area had a commanding general in charge of the soldiers in his area along the wall. In times of peace they guarded the part of the wall for which they were responsible; in times of war they placed themselves under the President of the Board of War or the imperial commissioner to manoeuvre or to support the other garrison areas. About 100,000 soldiers were stationed in each garrison area, depending on actual needs. Command headquarters was usually in one of the big towns along the wall.

Under the *zhen* was *lu* (pass) for the purpose of defence. The commander of each *lu* generally had his headquarters in an important pass. For instance, the Shanhaiguan Lu of the Ming period had a dozen passes under its jurisdiction, and its commander was stationed in Shanhaiguan.

Castles and passes were the important strategic points along the Great Wall, forming a defensive network and supporting neighbouring passes. Garrison commanders

The Great Wall crenelated on both sides.

The Great Wall in precipitous locations.

A fortification in the Great Wall.

A fortification (the square structure) in Dunhuang,
Gansu Province. It was inhabited by soldiers.

A round beacon tower.

Xinmingbao beacon tower outside Jiayuguan. At the base were materials for issuing the beacon smoke. Originally there were four containers on the platform for lighting the fires.

A now dilapidated watchtower that used to quarter soldiers.

A Han Dynasty reed torch, now exhibited in the Museum of Gansu Province.

A two-storey watchtower. The first floor was used to quarter soldiers and to store grain and weapons

Inside view of a watchtower.

Battlements for firing and observation.

Accessway to the wall.

An arched gateway in the inner side of the wall for soldiers going up or down.

Staircases for going up and down the tower.

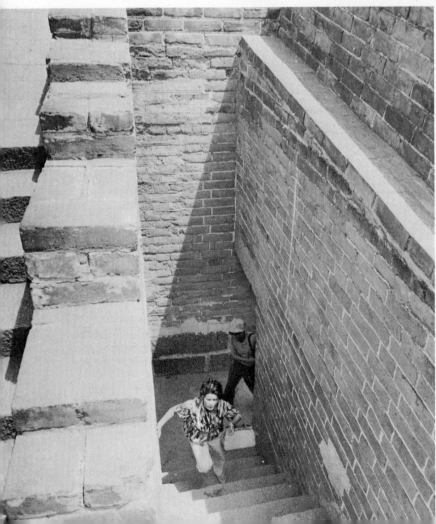

Steps leading from the arched gateway to the wall.

A stone drain trough
on   a   watchtower.

A drain on the wall.

Drain hole (the small square hole at the base).

Another stone drain trough.

Architectural and park experts from Beijing conducting an investigation at Badaling.

A piece of silk inscribed with "Addressing the commandant of Zhang Ye Prefecture," a Han Dynasty relic. It is now preserved in Zhang Ye Cultural Centre.

were stationed in important passes, and less important passes were guarded by minor officers. Garrison commanders did not have a definite number of soldiers under them. Shanhaiguan, Juyongguan and Jiayuguan were all guarded by a few hundred to a thousand soldiers.

Fortifications, the basic units of defence, were erected along the wall and also inside and outside the wall at vertical angles. The fortifications were equipped with beacon signals and guarded by soldiers numbering from a few dozen to a hundred and headed by officers at respective levels.

The beacon tower (also called smoke platform or signal tower) was used specifically for passing military information. A few soldiers were put on the towers in case of enemy attack.

Fighting towers, or platforms, were built on the wall for soldiers to watch out for and fight invading troops. The number of soldiers stationed on a tower varied from a few to 30, depending on the size of the tower.

As for the structure of the Great Wall, the wall itself was the major part of the construction. The style, method and structure varied from dynasty to dynasty. Even in one dynasty different kinds of wall were built. Take the relatively well preserved Ming Dynasty wall, for example. The part at Badaling near Beijing was very grand in the Ming Dynasty. The average height of the wall was 7 to 8 metres. Where the terrain was steep, the wall was lower — 3 to 5 metres. Where the ground was flatter, the wall was higher. The outer wall was higher than the inner one for greater defensive capability. The principle was to "take advantage of the steep terrain to construct defensive work." The average width of the base was 6.5 metres, of the top, only 5.8 metres; thus a cross section of the wall looks like a trapezium. That made the wall very stable. At intervals inside the wall there was an arched gate built of brick

or stone. Guards could go up or down the wall there. The stones used for the vaults, frames and thresholds of the gates were prefabricated and carried to the wall so as to build more quickly. The wall itself was built of stone slabs filled in with smaller stones and mortar, making it extremely solid.

The top of the wall was 3 or 4 layers of bricks — a surface of square bricks with 2 or 3 layers of bricks underneath it, sealed with white plaster. Wild grass could hardly grow on it. At particularly precipitous points it was hard to lay bricks, so staircases were built. The top of the wall was then about 4.5 metres, wide enough for 5 horses or 10 people to walk abreast. Near the inside wall a low wall of about one metre was built (also called parapet wall). On the outer wall were battlements about two metres high. Each battlement had one small hole for watching for enemy troops and another hole underneath it for shooting. A drain for rain water on top of the wall was connected to a long stone groove that extended beyond the wall to keep the water from washing the wall.

In other places, however, such as Liaodong, the Great Wall was built of rammed earth. Stone walls took advantage of the natural landscape; walls were carved out of mountain ridges or used steep cliffs as a defence screen. Walls were made of tree trunks or boards. Seven kinds altogether. At Jiayuguan there is also a wall made of a wooden fence on the mouth of a cliff. Ditches filled with water served as moats. The Han Dynasty wall at Yumenguan was built of tamarisk twigs and reeds filled with gravel.

Platforms protruding beyond the wall at almost the same level as the top of the wall, fitted with battlements, played an important role in fighting enemies. For instance, if enemy soldiers tried to climb the wall, guards could shoot from the wall and from both sides. Patrols stood guard there.

Some foundations can still be seen at Bada-ling. Called *pufang*, the battlemented platforms provided shelter for the patrols when it rained.

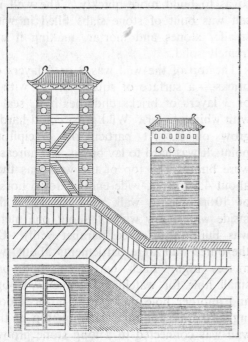

The platforms sat astride the wall and rose 2 to 3 stories above it. Guards could live in them, and they could also be used for storing weapons and ammunition. This type of platform was invented by the famous Ming general Qi Jiguang, who fought Japanese pirates in the latter half of the 16th century. In his *Records of Training Soldiers* he explains very clearly the process of building the platform and its functions. He says that the Great Wall was relatively low and thin and very easily collapsed. "The wall is occasionally faced with stone platforms. Soldiers cannot rescue one another in times of emergency. They are exposed to heat, wind, rain and cold. Weapons and ammunition are too far away to be sent there in time, and there is no place on the wall for storing large amounts of them. If an enemy outnumbers our soldiers and occupies high points and attack the wall from all

sides, it will be very difficult for the soldiers to defend the wall. Once there is a breakthrough on the wall, other soldiers will panic and flee. The enemy will then rush in to take the wall and there will be no way to stop them. Therefore, we are now building fortifications that are hollow inside. They will be built in places where it is easy for enemy troops to break through. These fortifications stand 9 to 12 metres high and 54 to 57 metres in perimeter. At strategic points a fortification is built every 10 to 100 steps; in less important places, every 150 to 200 steps; so that soldiers in these fortifications can always rescue one another. The foundation of the fortification is at the same level as the surface of the wall. It protrudes 5 metres beyond the wall on one side and 1.6 metres on the other side. The foundation's walls have holes for shooting arrows. A roof like that of a boat protects the guards, who can shoot at enemies below without being exposed to their arrows. Confronted with guns, enemy cavalrymen

General Qi Jiguang

dare not near the wall, so the defence is effective. One officer in every fortification is assigned to organize soldiers in fights. Two others are in charge of weapons and ammunition. The number of soldiers in each fortification varies from 30 to 50. A senior officer is in charge of 5 fortifications and a higher officer in charge of 10."

The fortifications that exist today from Shanhaiguan to Juyongguan began to be built in the time of Qi Jiguang. One kind, called horseback-fighting platform, has three stories and can store many weapons and much ammunition and house about 100 soldiers.

The beacon tower was used for sending information in times of enemy attack, smoke in the daytime and fire at night. The tower was a raised platform on which an observation room was built with materials and equipment for lighting the fire. Below the platform were a room where the guards lived and sheds for keeping sheep, horses, stores, etc. The structure of the tower was like that of the wall — some built of earth, some of rock, and some a combination of rocks and bricks. Beacon towers stood close to both sides of the wall, extended away from the wall outside it, extended towards the capital inside the wall, or connected with neighbouring counties, passes and garrison areas.

In the bamboo books of the Han Dynasty excavated in Dunhuang, Gansu Province, and in records of succeeding dynasties, there are detailed descriptions of the system of the beacon tower, including its position, structure, equipment and number of soldiers. Generally, beacon towers were built on mountain peaks and even on plains, wherever it was easy to observe other towers. Beacon towers near borders had walls to protect them. On every tower four chimneys were placed far enough apart so that they could be counted easily. The tower was stocked with swords, spears, bows and ar-

rows, dry weeds or firewood, wolf or cattle droppings, horses and dogs. Each tower had 5 to 10 soldiers, including a head and a vice-head. In times of peace one person stood guard, one cooked and the others collected firewood, or engaged in maintenance tasks.

Some ancient books contain particularly detailed accounts of the code and system of sending signals. It was decided in the Tang Dynasty (618-907) that, if the number of invaders ranged between 50 and 500, 1 torch should be lit; 2 torches if they numbered less than 3,000; 3 torches if they were on horseback, and the number ranged between 500 and 1,000; and 4 torches if they were between 1,000 and 10,000 but the exact number was not known. It was also decided that a one-torch signal should reach the county and prefecture in charge, and two-torch signals or above should all reach the capital. The prefecture, county or garrison area where the signals were originally sent should immediately send messengers on horseback to deliver the information to the court. The all-clear signal after the enemy's retreat was torches lit twice and extinguished twice. (See *A Collection of the Most Important Military Techniques* by Zeng Gongliang and others of the Song Dynasty.)

In the Ming Dynasty cannon shots were added to torches: "1 torch and 1 shot for a few enemies to 100; 2 torches and 2 shots for 500 enemies; 3 torches and 3 shots for over 1,000 enemies; 4 torches and 4 shots for over 5,000 enemies; 5 torches and 5 shots for over 10,000 enemies." (Decree issued in 1466, the second year of the Chenhua reign of the Ming Dynasty.)

Because of the importance of the delivery of military intelligence, emperors of every dynasty held very stringent control over it. Soldiers in charge of lighting torches must not leave their posts of their own accord, or they would be severely punished. According to a bamboo manuscript written in the

Han Dynasty, "The soldiers guarding the border areas are not allowed to move an inch from their posts." (From *Travelogue of Yumenguan*.)

Cheng, zhang, hou and bao were defensive structures inside and outside the wall, some along it, some farther away from it. These were not used for transmitting military intelligence but for defence. The *cheng*, a kind of wall, was built in coordination with the Great Wall. Several *chengs* were discovered near the site of the Qin and Han walls in Weichang County, Hebei Province. They were separated by several dozen kilometres. There were also small *chengs* extending away from the Great Wall inside and outside it. *Changs* were also a kind of wall but on a smaller scale. They are called "small walls amid the mountains" in some ancient documents. The major difference between a *cheng* and *zhang* was that *chengs* varied in size and were inhabited by civilians, whereas the *zhangs* were inhabited only by soldiers and varied little in size and form. The sites of four *zhangs* have been discovered in Inner Mongolia.

They were all squares with a perimeter of 450 metres, with a door only on one side. Platforms were built on the four corners of each building. One *zhang* had a fortification built over the door and a moat around it.

The *hou*, also called *chihou*, was a kind of raised platform for guards to keep watch on. It was relatively simple in construction and used with beacon towers.

The *bao* of the Ming Dynasty was much the same as the *zhang* in the Han Dynasty — also for defence purposes, often used in conjunction with passes and fortifications. A *bao* was usually surrounded by a wall and was also inhabited by people. Some *baos* also had beacon towers. Records show there was a *dun* (another kind of fortification) every 5 li and a *bao* every 10 li.

Guan, sai, ai and kou were built in strategic passes in valleys to block the enemy's route.

There were many such fortifications along the Great Wall. They were the key points of defence in times of war and key means of transportation in times of peace. Shanhaiguan and Juyongguan provide typical examples.

How the Great Wall Was Built

Such a gigantic and arduous project as the Great Wall required a tremendous amount of manpower and materials and very complicated design and construction.

The manpower necessary for building the Great Wall came from both soldiers and common people. The garrison constituted the main force. For example, the Great Wall in the time of Qin Shi Huang was built by 300,000 soldiers under General Meng Tian after he defeated the Xiongnu. It took them nine years to complete the construction. Even before Qin Shi Huang's time the princely states used soldiers as the main force for building walls.

Besides soldiers, Qin Shi Huang mobilized about 500,000 common people to build the Great Wall. In A.D. 555 the emperor of the Northern Qi Dynasty mobilized 1,800,000 people to build the part of the wall stretching from Nankou near Juyongguan to Datong, about 900 li. In 607 in the Sui Dynasty more than a million men were mobilized to build the wall; in 608 another 200,000 people were mobilized. When there were no men left, widows were compelled to join the construction work. Convicts were also included. In the Qin and Han dynasties a special penalty called *chengdan* forced criminals to labour at the construction site of the Great Wall as a form of punishment. According to *Records of the Historian*, Qin Shi Huang adopted, in 213 B.C., the suggestion of Li Si, the prime minister, and ordered all books of poetry and all books in general kept by the common people, except those on the history of Qin, medicine and tree planting, burned. Those who did not burn their books within 30 days were subjected to the *chengdan* penalty. Their heads would be shaved, their necks encircled with an iron ring and their faces tattooed and blackened before they were sent to build the wall. They also had to stand guard and patrol in turn. This kind of punishment lasted four years.

Rulers of succeeding generations also made up many excuses to force people to work on the wall.

The geographical conditions of the area where the Great Wall is located are rather varied, for it passes through steep mountains, deep valleys and rivers, deserts and grasslands. The military experts took advantage of natural conditions and chose places which are strategically located and difficult of access to build walls, passes and beacon towers.

"Using the steep and difficult terrain to guard the passes" was the dictum in Qin Shi Huang's time, adopted by every dynasty thereafter. Present-day remains indicate that passes were usually built between two mountain peaks, at the meeting of two river valleys, or along key roads on the plains. In this way manpower and materials could be saved and the strategically important places guarded. Sites for beacon towers and fortifications were more carefully selected. Beacon towers were built on mountaintops or open country, so that signals for rescue could be observed in time.

Examples of taking advantage of the natural terrain to build walls can be found everywhere. For instance, the Badaling wall near Juyongguan was built along a mountain ridge. The ridge made the wall steeper and harder to attack. In some places the slope is very steep on the outside but relatively flat inside, because the outside was for blocking the enemy, whereas the inside was for the guards to walk about. Huge rocks and cliffs were already fit for fortifications, needing only a few changes. Where there were precipitous cliffs, the wall would stop, for the cliffs were fortifications in themselves. Walls also made use of huge rivers and deep valleys for defensive purposes.

Since the wall stretched over great distances, management of construction was extremely complicated. Responsibility for different parts of the wall coordinated with defence. For instance, the four prefectures of the Han Dynasty west of the Yellow River (Wuwei, Zhangye, Jiuquan and Dunhuang) divided the task among themselves. The major projects and passes were built by the forces organized by the prefectures. The central government also mobilized troops and civilians to work in key sites.

On the Great Wall at Badaling a stone tablet recording construction of the wall in the Ming Dynasty during the 10th year (1582) of the reign of Wanli was discovered.

It can be seen from this tablet that several thousand soldiers, along with many common people, built just over 220 metres of wall and a stone arch gate. These soldiers were assigned from Shandong — a very far province.

Most of the building materials were taken from the site. Before bricks were used in large amounts, the main materials were wood and tiles, earth and stones. On high mountains stones were used, while on the plains earth was used. In desert areas walls were built of reeds and tamarisk twigs layered with sand. The Han wall at Yumenguan, Gansu Province, was built this way. First a layer of reeds or tamarisk branches, then a layer of sand, then another layer of reeds or tamarisk branches, until the wall reached 5 to 6 metres. Reed or tamarisk layers were about 5 centimetres thick and sand layers about 20 centimetres, so a 5-metre wall needed about 20 layers of sand and reeds or tamarisk branches. The Liaodong wall was built of oakwood and boards.

Many key parts of the Ming Dynasty Great Wall were built of bricks and stones, so large amounts of bricks and lime were needed. These were made in kilns set up on the spot. The wood needed for building passes, castles and watchtowers was obtained in nearby areas. If there were no trees nearby, it would have to be transported from afar. The construction organization for each section of the wall also established its own supply departments, quarries and kilns. Since the demand for building materials was great, the staff of the supply departments was also great.

Without modern machinery and transportation, construction was incredibly difficult. The walls in Juyongguan and Badaling are built of 3-metre-long stone slabs weighing over 1,000 kilogrammes apiece. Since the walls were built along steep mountain ranges, it was strenuous work even to carry large bricks weighing dozens of kilogrammes each and huge quantities of lime.

Before building the wall, workers had to find the "level" — that is, laying the slabs so that the pressure was spread evenly and the wall wouldn't collapse.

Transportation was a major problem. Workers and technicians created many ways to carry uphill large quantities of earth, lime, huge stone slabs and big bricks.

The most primitive way was to use hands, baskets, or shoulder poles. Sometimes the workers stood in a row and passed bricks uphill one by one. They did the same with baskets of lime. This saved climbing up and down the mountains; it also prevented

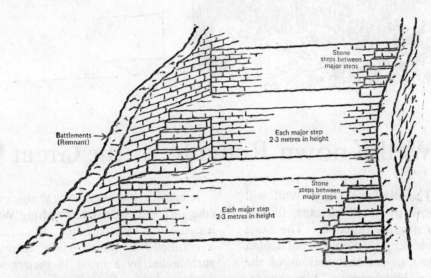

DIAGRAM OF STONE STAIRCASE WALL AT DADIANZI OUTSIDE SHANHAIGUAN PASS

The wall was built this way: First two outside walls were built, then the space between was filled in. When the wall reached a certain height, bricks were laid on top, either at a slant or on the level. If the wall did not slant too much, the bricks could be slanted, whereas if the wall exceeded 45 degrees, the bricks had to be level. One section of the Great Wall outside Shanhaiguan is composed of two steps, one 1 metre high, the other 3 metres high. Smaller steps make it possible for people to climb.

people from bumping into one another, especially when paths were narrow.

On even ground and not too steep slopes, wheelbarrows were used, while in deep valleys and ditches, workers rigged up ropes and slid baskets of bricks and lime along them.

It is recorded that in Badaling donkeys carried baskets of lime up the mountains and bricks were tied to the horns of goats, which were lured up the mountains.

Some Well-Known Remains of the Great Wall

The Ten Thousand Li Great Wall will forever remain a treasured heritage, though it has lost its original function. The State Council of the People's Republic of China decided in 1961 to put the sections of the Great Wall in Shanhaiguan, Juyongguan, Badaling and Jiayuguan under state protection as important historical monuments. Over the years the wall has been repaired and opened to the public. Walls built in succeeding dynasties in various provinces and cities are under the protection of governments at different levels.

Shanhaiguan

Shanhaiguan is situated in the northeastern part of Qinhuangdao City in northern Hebei Province at the end of Bohai Bay. It borders on mountains and faces the sea, forming a pass of strategic importance at the eastern end of the Great Wall in the Ming Dynasty.

It became known as Shanhaiguan in 1381 (the 14th year of Emperor Hong Wu), when a castle was erected here. It's square, with a perimeter of about 4,000 metres, and is surrounded by a moat 18 metres wide and 8 metres deep. Each side has a gate. There are also fortifications to the east and west. The Great Wall extends from the castle to the east, to the west, to the south until it reaches the sea and to the north to meet the Yanshan Mountains. Not far from the pass, on the south and north wings, are fortifications where soldiers were stationed. Outside Shanhaiguan's east gate are many fortifications and towers. Remains of the outer fortification, called Weiyuan, and of the Balibao Tower (a beacon tower) still exist. Far from being a solitary castle, Shanhaiguan, depending on the steep mountains and the sea, formed a complete defence system with inner and outer walls, towers and fortifications.

The arched east gate, built on a high foundation, leads to the outside of the pass.

Huanghuacheng Great Wall in
Huairou County, Beijing.

Chu Great Wall, built of rocks.

Ming Great Wall, built of rocks.

Qin Great Wall, built of earth.

Section of Jinshanling Great Wall with brick on both sides and rock and loess inside.

The Great Wall and a beacon tower built of reed, tamarisk, sand and rock.

Tower built of rocks.

Part of the tower with an inscription "Ten-thousand-*ren**-high cliff" written by Ma Yong, commander of the Liaodong Garrison Area of the Ming Dynasty.

* *Ren* — an ancient measure of length equal to seven or eight feet.

A brick from the Ming Great Wall.

Part of the brick with the inscription "Made by the Tartar-Quelling Battalion in the sixth year of the Wanli reign."

Stone tablet bearing the names of the builders of Jiayuguan Great Wall in the Jiaqing reign of the Ming Dynasty.

Section of a staircase-like wall built on steep slopes in Suizhong County, Liaoning Province.

The Great Wall in Luanping County, Hebei Province.

Beacon-tower defence line. In the Zhuizi Mountains, where Hebei and Liaoning meet, the terrain is steep and inaccessible. With the mountains as barriers, people in ancient times built beacon towers on the peaks to signal an enemy attack — smoke in the daytime and fire at night.

Gubeikou Great Wall 30 years ago.

Erdaoguan Pass at Huanghuacheng in Huairou County, Beijing.

Two watchtowers at the mouth of a valley in Mentougou on the western outskirts of Beijing.

Snares for trapping horses outside Jiayuguan.

A castle of the Ming Great Wall, in Weiyuan County, Gansu.

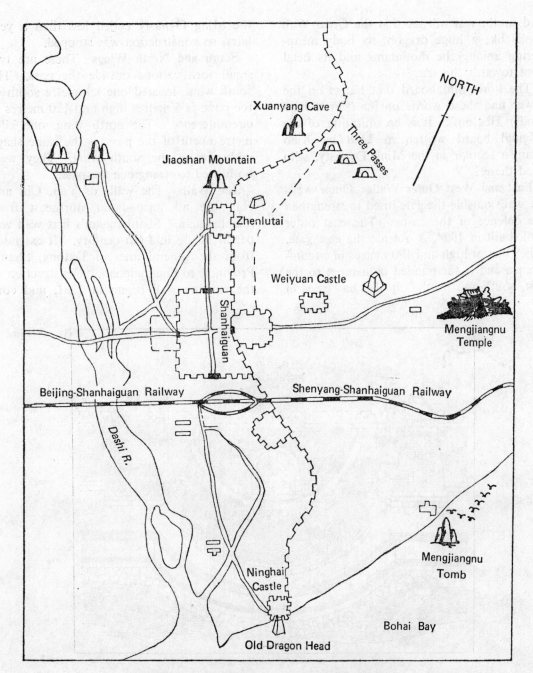

NORTH

Xuanyang Cave

Three Passes

Jiaoshan Mountain

Zhenlutai

Weiyuan Castle

Shanhaiguan

Mengjiangnu Temple

Beijing-Shanhaiguan Railway

Shenyang-Shanhaiguan Railway

Dashi R.

Mengjiangnu Tomb

Ninghai Castle

Bohai Bay

Old Dragon Head

SKETCH MAP OF SHANHAIGUAN PASS

There was also a drawbridge outside the gate and another square wall that strengthened the defensive power. The gatetower is a 3-room, 2-story building 10 metres high, 17 metres wide at the top and 27 metres wide at the bottom. There are 68 shooting holes on the east, south and north sides. If you climb up the tower and look north and south, you will see that the Great Wall looks like a huge dragon, its body meandering among the mountains and its head bent towards the sea.

The horizontal board that hangs on the tower had these words on it: "First Pass Under Heaven." It is an imitation of the original board written in 1448 by Xiao Xian, a scholar in the Ming Dynasty, who lived there.

East and West Outer Walls Outer walls are walls outside the gate, used to strengthen the defence of the castle. The east outer wall, built in 1584, is outside the east gate. It is 8 metres high and 180 metres in circumference and is surrounded by a moat to the east, south and north. It also has gates in

the Ming Dynasty ended less than a year later, so construction was stopped.

South and North Wings These are two small fortifications outside the pass. The south wing, located one kilometre south of the pass, is 6 metres high and 120 metres in circumference. The north wing, one kilometre north of the pass, is the same shape and size as the south wing. They were both used to strengthen the pass.

The Walls The walls of Yan, Qin and Han are all located far northeast from Shanhaiguan. Shanhaiguan's first wall was begun in the mid-6th century. It extended from the general area of Datong, Shanxi Province, to Shanhaiguan. Construction of the existing wall began in 1381, and con-

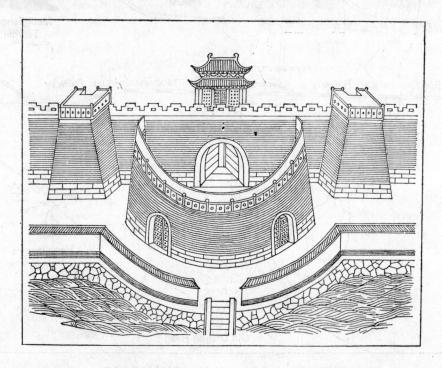

the south and north, two water gates, two corner towers and seven watchtowers. On the east gate are inscribed the three characters for Shanhaiguan, also written in the Ming Dynasty. The west outer wall, outside the west gate, was begun in 1643, but

tinued over the succeeding years. It is mainly bricks, filled in with rocks and rammed earth. Some parts are completely rocks. The wall's average height is about 7 metres, although some parts are as high as 14 metres.

Old Dragon Head and Chenghailou Tower
The Great Wall goes four kilometres from
the east gate of Shanhaiguan directly south
to the sea. This is called Old Dragon
Head. Not far from it is the foundation for
Chenghailou Tower, which was destroyed
long ago, except for many huge rectangular
stone slabs lying at the bottom of the sea.
The watchtower and foundations of Old
Dragon Head, reaching into the sea, are
very solid, built by the famous Ming Dynasty
general Qi Jiguang, who resisted Japanese
pirates. How is it that the foundations of
Old Dragon Head have remained intact for
several hundred years? Because a lot of
iron pots were put at the bottom of the sea,
reducing the wash of the waves.

The Great Wall of Jiaoshan Mountain To
the north of First Pass Under Heaven the
Great Wall extends for about 2.5 kilometres
to reach the foot of the Yanshan Mountains.
Then it winds its way up, spreading out into
many towers and fortifications on its way.
The wall encircles a mountain called Jiaoshan, hence its name Jiaoshan Great Wall.
Standing on top of the mountain, one can
overlook the wall and the sea; the view of
the sunrise from there is particularly pic-
turesque.

Outside Jiaoshan Great Wall a beacon
tower on top of the mountain to the east is
still in good condition.

Three Passes and Xuanyang Cave About
five kilometres to the northeast of Shanhaiguan are three passes along the Great Wall,
the first built at the mouth of a stream, the
second at the foot of a mountain, and the
third in the middle of the mountain. It
is so steep that looking up one feels as
though the Great Wall were built on top of
a sheer cliff.

Above the Three Passes in the middle of
Huangniu Mountain is Xuanyang Cave.
The cave is dim and narrow at first, then
gradually it gets wider and brighter. In
the roof of the cave is an opening through
which one can look, hence its name Seeing
the Sky from Inside the Cave. It is one of
the most beautiful spots in Shanhaiguan.

Meng Jiangnü Temple Also called Zhen-
nü (Devoted Wife) Temple, it is located
6.5 kilometres east of Shanhaiguan and is
said to have been built before the 13th
century.

Mention of the Ten Thousand Li Great
Wall often leads to the story of Meng Jiangnü. (See also the section called "Legends
of the Great Wall.") For a long time people used the story of Meng Jiangnü to ex-
pose the cruelty of Qin Shi Huang towards
the labouring people and express their dissatisfaction with the ruling class.

One version of the story goes like this:
Meng Jiangnü and her husband, Fan
Qiliang, lived on the bank of the Yellow
River in Shaanxi Province. Soon after they
were married, Fan was forced to go to build
the Great Wall and stayed there for over 10
years. Meng Jiangnü missed her husband
day and night. Finally she made some
clothes for him and went to the Great Wall
to look for him, but her husband had died
long ago and was buried under the wall.
Meng Jiangnü cried and cried, until her
tears caused the wall to collapse and she saw
her husband's bones. The story reached
Qin Shi Huang, and he ordered Meng Jiangnü brought to him so he could punish her.
When he saw her, however, he changed his
mind and wanted her instead to become his
concubine. Meng Jiangnü demanded that
her husband be reburied with proper ceremony, and the emperor agreed. After the
ceremony, the emperor and Meng Jiangnü
went boating on Bohai. Meng Jiangnü,
cursing the emperor, jumped into the sea.
Since then she has been revered as a loyal
and dedicated wife who dared to fight against
a cruel ruler. People pay their respects to
her every year.

In reality, the Ten Thousand Li Great
Wall of Qin Shi Huang's time is several

hundred li north of Shanhaiguan, and the story of Meng Jiangnü is based on the story of a woman who went looking for her husband a few hundred years before Qin Shi Huang. The husband, Qiliang, lived at the end of the 5th, or the beginning of the 6th, century B.C. He was forced to perform corvée service and died before his wife went to look for him. Later people confused the two stories, creating the story of Meng Jiangnü looking for her husband and crying down the Great Wall. The story has passed from one generation to another.

Today the temple has a front gate, front hall, rear hall and pavilion. Beside the rear hall are two huge rocks on which are carved "Stone of Expecting the Husband" and a poem written by the Qing emperor Qian Long extolling Meng Jiangnü. Standing on the rocks, people can see the sea in the south and the Yanshan Mountains in the north, with the Great Wall meandering along the mountain slopes.

Several rocks protruding from the sea south of Meng Jiangnü Temple are said to be her tomb. Because of their steepness, nobody can scale them, but flocks of birds land on them. It is another interesting feature of Shanhaiguan.

Gubeikou

A section of the Great Wall several dozen kilometres in length was discovered in Bakeshiying Commune, Luanping County, Hebei Province, after a joint investigation by the State Administration of Historical Relics and the Ministry of Culture. This part of the wall is well preserved and is equal in scale and grandeur to the Badaling Great Wall near Beijing, so people refer to it as the Second Badaling. It is actually called Shalingkou, also known as Jingshanling, and is a component part of the defence system in the Gubeikou area.

It was not until A.D. 555 that Gubeikou had its first Great Wall, built by Northern Qi from Shaanxi to Shanhaiguan, covering over 3,000 li. (The walls of the Warring States Period and Qin and Han dynasties were built far to its north.) Since the Gubeikou Great Wall was built of earth and stones and was low and small in scale, there are hardly any remains. Gubeikou began to be a strategic pass in the Ming Dynasty. Like Juyongguan, it was an important gateway to the Ming capital of Beijing. Therefore, strong fortifications were built and many soldiers were stationed there. The newly discovered Shalingkou Great Wall was a subordinate pass for Gubeikou.

In the Qing Dynasty Gubeikou remained an important passage to the Mongolian grasslands and the northeastern region, even though the building of walls had stopped. After Emperor Kang Xi built the Summer Resort in Chengde, Gubeikou became a place Qing emperors must pass through on their way to Chengde.

From a watchtower on the highest peak near Gubeikou, along the Great Wall, one can see Beijing on a fine day or its lights at night. Hence it is called Tower for Watching Beijing. On the Shalingkou Great Wall there is another tower, called Flower Tower, with a marble arch gate. Inside the gate a stone tablet records the building of the Great Wall in the Ming Dynasty.

South of the Gubeikou Great Wall there is a lake with a high dam — Miyun Reservoir — which is a major source of water for Beijing as well as a popular scenic spot. If Miyun Reservoir, Gubeikou and Shalingkou walls, and the Summer Resort in Chengde were linked together, the Gubeikou-Shalingkou area would become an important scenic spot for tourists.

Juyongguan

Juyongguan is located in a 15-kilometre

valley 50 kilometres northwest of Beijing. The valley leads from Inner Mongolia and Shanxi to Beijing.

According to research, poor labourers were settled here during the reign of Qin Shi Huang, hence its name, Juyongguan, or Pass Where Common People Live. However, the wall built in Qin Shi Huang's time did not pass here, but reached Liaodong from far north instead. While building the Great Wall, Qin Shi Huang established 12 prefectures along the wall to guarantee supplies for the development of nearby areas. Among them was Shanggu Prefecture, located near today's Juyongguan. It is possible, therefore, that some people migrated there during the reign of Qin Shi Huang.

A wall was built near Juyongguan in 446 during the Northern Wei Dynasty. In 555 the Northern Qi built a wall from Nankou near Juyongguan to Datong in Shanxi, ranging over 900 li. Then the wall went from there to Shanhaiguan in the east. Thus, Juyongguan was connected with the Great Wall, becoming an important pass.

The present-day Juyongguan fortifications and walls were rebuilt in the Ming Dynasty.

After the Yuan Dynasty was replaced by the Ming, the Ming court sent General Xu Da to build passes at Juyongguan and other places. After 1450 it again had Juyongguan repaired and sent troops to guard it. Today, on the board over the gate with the three characters for Juyongguan written on it, one can still see "Erected in the fifth year of the Jingtai reign [1454] on an auspicious day in August." It is also recorded in the *Documentary Records of Emperor Ying Zong*: "Construction of Juyongguan was completed in the sixth month of the sixth year of the Jingtai reign [1455]."

In the Yuan Dynasty the emperor often passed through Juyongguan going from Dadu (modern Beijing) to Shangdu (Upper Capital, in modern Inner Mongolia). Inside the castle were temples, gardens and residences for the emperor. At the northern and southern ends of the castle were two huge red gates. The southern gate was within today's Nankou, the northern in the vicinity of today's Badaling. An elaborate tower-like overpass was built inside the pass in the Yuan Dynasty. In the south and north ends of the castle two garrison headquarters were set up, manned by 3,000 soldiers, mainly for patrolling at night to prevent robbery and theft.

Juyongguan of the Ming Dynasty had two gates, one in water and one on dry land. Nowadays, only the one on dry land remains. In the Ming Dynasty the overpass was within the castle. In the castle were Tai'an Temple, offices for civil and military officers, barracks, and a grand library. Today, remains of the temple and library can still be seen.

Juyongguan is in a very long valley with an outpost at the southern and northern ends; the southern outpost (called Nankou), over 40 kilometres from Beijing, was the entrance to the valley; the northern outpost was the Badaling pass. Juyongguan is in between, and between Juyongguan and Badaling are the remains of a pass, called Shangguan, built by Xu Da at the beginning of the Ming Dynasty.

Because Juyongguan was in a narrow, deep valley with steep mountain slopes on both sides and gates at the north and south ends guarded by large numbers of soldiers, it was called "absolutely safe fortification" or "unconquerable fortification." Over the centuries it witnessed many battles.

Caught between mountains in a river valley, Juyongguan opens into a valley of over 30 li. Bubbling streams, tree-covered slopes and birds singing in the forests make it one of the most beautiful spots in the northwestern part of Beijing. As early as the Kin Dynasty, 800 years ago, it was considered one of the eight famous scenic spots in Beijing, then called Yanjing. The valley was said to contain 72 sights, such as the Rock for Watching Beijing, Heavenly Fortification, Five Devil Heads, and Fairy Bridge.

Cloud Terrace at Juyongguan Cloud Terrace (Yun Tai), originally an overpass built in 1345 across a street but later only a platform, was within the castle of the Ming Juyongguan. A low white marble balustrade surrounds a high stone platform with a deep gate and vivid carvings, constituting an elaborate work of art.

SKETCH MAP OF THE MING DYNASTY JUYONGGUAN PASS

Qingzi No. 15 Barracks

Yongzi No. 8 Barracks

Zhenguan Fortification

Badaling

Zhenguan Fortification

Juyongguan

Nankou

Houxiangkou

Beacon tower

Cloud Terrace was built in the Yuan Dynasty, but its gate has an arch with eight angles, the shape of city gates before the Yuan and Song dynasties. Surrounding the platform are water outlets in the shape of a dragon head. Railings around the foundation are decorated with pearls and animal images. On top of the platform are the foundations of five rooms dating back to the Ming period. These are the remains of the Tai'an Temple built in the Ming Dynasty.

Carved on both sides of the platform's gateway are images of Lamaism, such as the four heavenly kings and "six snares," images of six animals. Covering the wall between the four heavenly kings are Buddhist scriptures in Sanskrit, Tibetan, Mongolian, Uygur, Han and Xixia languages. There is also a record of the construction of Cloud Terrace in the Han language. That these languages are carved in the same place shows that cultural exchanges were taking place among the various nationalities of China in the Yuan Dynasty. They are also important material for the study of ancient writings.

Badaling

Badaling is situated at the northern entrance to Juyongguan valley. From Badaling one can command a bird's-eye view of Juyongguan and also see Beijing.

Badaling, like Juyongguan, is also caught between mountains with a valley. There is a small castle at the end. The Great Wall was built to the north and south up the mountains. The castle is rectangular, with a gate on the east and west sides. From available historical records and the inscribed boards and stone tablets in the castle, it can be concluded that the Badaling Great Wall underwent almost 80 years of construction, from 1505 to 1582. On the outer gatetower in Juyongguan a stone tablet from

1582 tells about building the Badaling Great Wall and watchtowers. It also records the names of the officers and the number of workers involved in the construction. The tablet refers to "second captain for the defence of the Badaling area." Officers of this rank were in charge of important passes along the Great Wall and other military strongholds and were subordinate to a brigadier-general; they could also control patrols in that area. Under him were three sergeants, one police inspector and 788 soldiers spread around the passes, watchtowers and the wall itself. Their weapons included armour, tiger-skin hats, huge swords, daggers, shields, bows and arrows, cannon, lead bullets, gunpowder and equipment for lighting signals.

Because of its steep landscape and strong defence, the Badaling Great Wall was seldom attacked directly. Beijing was usually seized in a roundabout way from Nankou.

The Badaling Great Wall belongs to the inner wall. Another wall along Zhangjiakou, Wanquan, Chicheng and Yanggao can be seen from Badaling.

At the former station of Qinglongqiao under Badaling there is a pavilion with a stone tablet and bronze statue commemorating Zhan Tianyou. Zhan Tianyou went to study in the United States when he was young and, after his return, took part in building railways. The Badaling section of the Beijing to Zhangjiakou railway was so dangerous that even foreign companies dared not take on the design and construction. After careful investigation Zhan Tianyou created the Z-shape way of going uphill, thus solving the problem of steep slopes. This section of the railway, laid between 1905 and 1909, became one of the world's great engineering feats. The Chinese people respected Zhan and, therefore, erected a memorial. In 1982 the Ministry of Railways of the People's Republic of China built a new tomb behind the statue and also held a solemn ceremony to rebury the ashes of Zhan Tianyou and his wife.

Yanmenguan

Yanmenguan is an important pass along the outer Great Wall, 20 kilometres to the northwest of Daixian County, Shanxi Province. Everything except the arched gate was destroyed long ago.

Hengshan Mountain to the west and the famous Wutai Mountain to the southeast face each other, forming the shape of a gate. It is recorded in *Classics of Mountains and Rivers*: "Yanmen means that swallows fly out the gate." Hence its name, Yanmenguan, or Swallow Gate Pass.

The construction of Yanmenguan began in the Tang Dynasty. In 1374 a castle was built on its present site.

The Great Wall meanders along Yanmenguan. Like a jade belt, it links the mountain peaks together. It is furnished with beacon towers, fortifications and watchtowers. Outside the pass there used to be three huge stone walls, 25 small stone walls and 18 openings. Yanmenguan, Ningwuguan and Piantouguan are called the Outer Three Passes.

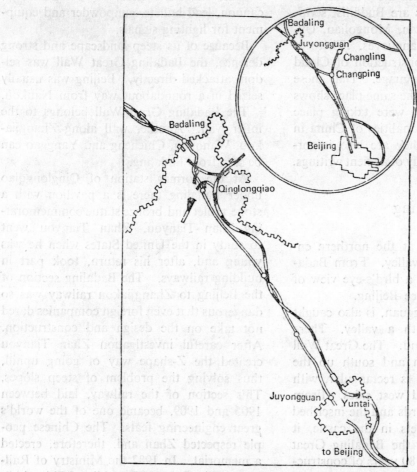

SKETCH MAP OF JUYONGGUAN AND BADALING

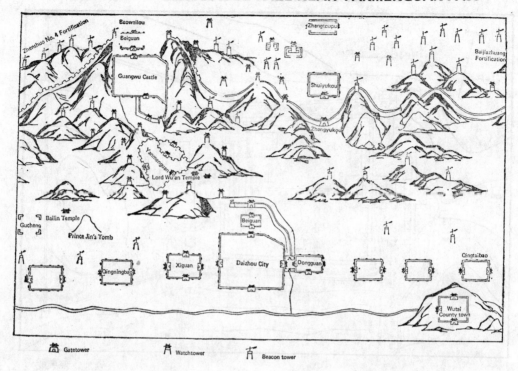

Gatetower   Watchtower   Beacon tower

Yanmenguan has always been fought over. In 980 the Song Dynasty general Yang Ye guarded it and defeated the Liao troops. In 1937, during the War of Resistance Against Japan, the Eighth Route Army, later known as the People's Liberation Army, lay in ambush there for the Japanese troops and won brilliant victories.

Ningwuguan and Pianguan

The present-day Ningwu County in Shanxi Province was the site of Ningwuguan in ancient times.

Built in 1450, Ningwuguan is located in the middle of the Outer Three Passes, a strategic point between east and west. The pass lies in the intersection of four mountains and could support Yanmen in the east and Pianguan in the west.

Pianguan, also called Piantouguan, is in today's Pianguan County, Shanxi Province. The pass was built following the landscape, high in the east and low in the west, looking like a head turned to one side, hence its another name, *piantou*, meaning head inclined to one side. Begun in 1389, it was rebuilt many times in the Ming Dynasty. In 1466 four walls, ranging from 30 to 70 kilometres, were built. Overlooking the Yellow River, the walls look magnificent.

Jiayuguan

Jiayuguan, the best preserved of all the passes of the Great Wall, is in the western part of the Gansu Corridor of Gansu Province. It was the western end of the Ming Great Wall, a strategic point in ancient times.

The castle and the Great Wall were begun

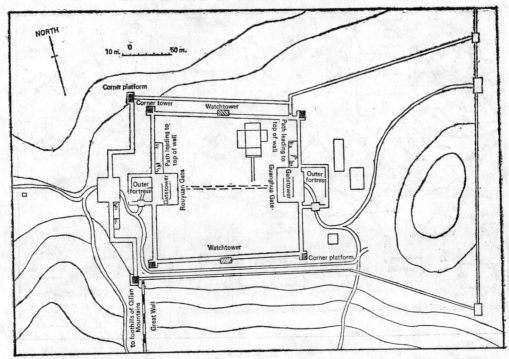

in 1372. They were built of rammed earth, therefore very solid. A highway west from today's Jiuquan City cuts through the Gobi Desert for a few dozen kilometres directly to the foot of Jiayuguan. The highway was built along the ancient road, so one can see beacon towers rising high on both sides of the road — a small tower every 2.5 kilometres and a big one every 5 kilometres. The castle itself towers overhead. To the south are the snowcapped Qilian Mountains with the Great Wall extending to their foot. To the north is the boundless Gobi Desert. In front of the pass a clear stream waters several hundred *mu* of rice fields. The stretch of green adds to the beauty of the pass on the Gobi Desert.

The pass is shaped like a trapezoid, big at the west end and small at the east. The east wall is about 154 metres long, the west about 166 metres, the north and south about 160 metres. Outside the west wall there is another thick wall, making the defence in the west particularly solid. Another low rammed-earth wall starts from the western end of the outer wall and encircles the pass, paralleling the south and north walls. To the east of the pass another rammed-earth wall encloses a square. Outside the castle wall, there are also triangular snares for trapping horses.

The pass has eastern and western gates, both of which have towers on top. Near the eastern gate are a stage, temple, palace and other structures. Outside the western gate there was a gate to the outer wall that served as the main entrance to Jiayuguan. The horizontal board with the characters for First Pass Under Heaven used to be above this gate. The gate was destroyed before Liberation. Inside the pass the northern sides of the eastern and western

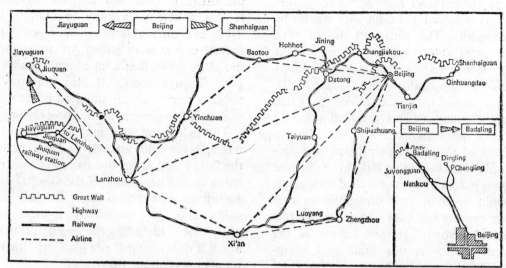

SKETCH MAP OF TRANSPORTATION ROUTES FROM BEIJING
TO SHANHAIGUAN, BADALING AND JIAYUGUAN

gates have wide roads leading to the top of the wall.

On the four corners of the castle are brick towers two stories high built in the shape of fortifications. In the middle of the southern and northern walls are watchtowers. On the northern and southern ends of the west side of the outer wall are corner platforms on which towers were built. From the top of the castle one can get a bird's-eye view of the whole construction in full grandeur.

The major part of the castle is rammed earth. Only gatetowers and corner towers are brick. The wall is 10.6 metres high, 5 metres thick at the bottom and 2 metres thick at the top, so the top is much narrower than the foundation. Crenels were built on the outside of the wall, and a low rammed-earth wall supports the main wall, making it extremely solid. The western side of the outer wall was built of brick completely because it faced the enemy.

Remaining inside the pass are a garrison commander's office built in the Qing Dynasty and a well pavilion. Barracks and storerooms for grain and weapons were destroyed long ago.

Although the Great Wall near Jiayuguan is broken, its construction is still visible. Most of the wall is rammed earth, about six metres high. The wall takes four different forms: without crenels, largely used in places not easily accessible to enemies; with crenels and a platform for soldiers to patrol, used at strategic points; built of logs and boards along precipices; and a special form for low-lying and water-logged places. It was 10 metres wide and stopped at the water. The bottom was 3.3 square metres. It was flanked by two dams of rammed earth 1.6 metres high, the bottom 1.3 metres and the top 0.5 metre.

Jiayuguan had 39 beacon towers under its control. A fortification on the way from Jiayuguan to Jiuquan is surrounded by a square wall. Its door opens to the south. The buildings inside, providing lodging for several dozen people, have mostly been destroyed, leaving only one beacon tower standing. It is built of earth in the shape of a taper, about six metres high. Steps at the back lead to the top.

Documents record many kinds of platforms for the Ming Dynasty Great Wall.

A Ming stone tablet records: "Huge fortifications were ordered built with platforms in the middle. The platforms should have arched gates and overline bridges. Walls should be erected around the fortifications and hidden iron doors built into the walls. Big guns should be placed behind the gates and crenels made. This is called iron city capable of quick attacks.... According to the form of the above-mentioned fortification a platform should be built in the middle and guns placed under the arched iron gates. It should open in four directions so that soldiers can use big guns and other firearms to attack enemies. Houses on top of the platform are for storing grain and equipment. At the bottom of the platform are many wells for protracted engagements.... The layout of another kind of platform is like this: one platform in the middle, with two solid platforms and two hollow ones on its four corners. The hollow ones have crenels for firing guns. There are also ladders for soldiers to climb up to and down from the platform. Hidden weapons and triangle snares for trapping horses were prepared...."

In the exhibition halls at Jiuquan and Zhangye are many historical relics from Jiayuguan, including a stone tablet recording the building of Jiayuguan in 1437. There is also a piece of wood with an order carved on it:

> The Jiayuguan garrison commander's office grants the holder of the order the right to go out of the pass to Liugou to collect grain. But if, when he returns, there is a substitute or covering for escaped convicts and it is found out, he shall be severely punished.
> Issued in the 56th year of Kang Xi

From this order one can see the pass system for Jiayuguan at the beginning of the Qing Dynasty. The Liugou mentioned in the order is over 300 li from Jiayuguan. It was a key passageway to Qinghai and Tibet and also a large grain depot. That special orders were issued for travelling to the place shows that a lot of grain must have gone through there. It also indicates the military and political situation in the northwest at the beginning of the Qing Dynasty.

The exhibition also includes a lot of armour, bows and arrows, and big guns of the Ming and Qing dynasties. From mid-Ming to the beginning of the Qing Dynasty Jiayuguan had 170 soldiers in exile or in shifts and 343 mobilized soldiers — 513 altogether. Including the 39 platforms with about a dozen guards per platform, the total number was about 1,000.

Remains of the Lintao Great Wall

Lintao is within the territory of Minxian County, southern Gansu Province, on the bank of the Taohe River. Fertile land borders the river, very favourable for the development of agriculture and animal husbandry. Many famous remains dating from Chinese primitive society are scattered along the river banks. Lintao was one of the strategic points for the feudal ruling class of succeeding dynasties. Qin Shi Huang sent Meng Tian and his troops to build the Great Wall, the west end of which was Lintao.

The Qin Great Wall is located on Great Wall Slope to the east of today's Lintao County. On top of the slope a section of wall over 400 metres long is still relatively well preserved. For over 200 metres the wall goes along the mountain ridge, crosses the valley and heads south. According to local people, there used to be a section of the wall on the opposite mountain, but no trace of it can be found today. To the north there are also over 200 metres of wall going up the mountain ridge. The wall is hardly distinguishable at the top of the mountain. Parts of the wall have collapsed or been destroyed by efforts to expand cultivated land. However, if you look far on top of the mountains, you can still make out the Great Wall meandering along the ridges like a dragon.

The remains of the Great Wall on the slope include:

The Great Wall Opening This is a huge broken gap. One can see a layer of earth at the bottom about 1.5 metres high, then a layer of loess rammed solid, about 3 metres thick and 10 metres wide. On top of that is an earth wall 2 metres high and 3.5 metres thick. Its rammed-earth layers are 6 cm to 10 cm thick. The structure is the same for the walls on both sides of the gap.

The wall South and north of the Great Wall Opening sections of the wall are still preserved. The wall was originally 2.5 metres high, 2 metres wide at the top and 3.6 metres wide at the base. The rammed earth is loess mixed with crushed stones. The section of the wall we see has collapsed at the top, forming a cone. Now it is 2.8 metres high, 2.9 metres wide at the bottom and 6 to 9 cm thick. One can see that the rammed earth is very irregular, about 3 or 4 cm in diameter, indicating that workers at that time used the primitive way of ramming earth.

Broken pieces of pottery Near the opening broken pottery tiles, pipes and containers can be seen everywhere. Inhabitants of the area say they often find unbroken tiles as large as half a metre in the wheat fields. One commune member had a tile as long as 49 cm. Though it was not complete, the original tile could be restored. The broken tiles, pipes and containers have been identified by archaeologists as products of the state of Qin in the Warring States Period. They resemble the Qin Dynasty tiles unearthed in today's Xi'an. From those pottery pieces we can determine that this was the original site of the Qin Great Wall.

The Han Great Wall at Yumenguan and Remains of the Beacon Towers

Yumenguan is situated 80 kilometres northwest of Dunhuang County in today's Gansu Province. Yumenguan and Yangguan to its south formed two major lines that led to the Western Regions in the Han Dynasty. There are hardly any remains of Yangguan, but remains of Yumenguan are still visible.

Square Fortification In the past scholars at home and abroad thought that Square Fortification was Yumenguan. In recent years, however, archaeologists in Gansu Province discovered remains of a castle five kilometres to the west of Yumenguan. It is possible that the gate to Yumenguan is to the west of Square Fortification. However, there is no doubt that the fortification was a part of the defence system of Yumenguan, for a pass is not just one fortification, but may be a series of fortifications. For instance, Juyongguan had three fortifications 15 kilometres apart.

Square Fortification is located between two mountains south and north where the Shule River flows. The river has an underground source and forms a small lake. The fortification is on the south bank of the lake. These natural conditions were the basis for the ancient Yumenguan, providing the soldiers and horses with water. The Great Wall stretches to the east and west 2.5 kilometres north of the river, protecting Yumenguan and this land of water and pasture. Other buildings related to the castle were distroyed, leaving only an earthen fortification.

The fortification is nearly square: 23 metres from west to east and 23.6 metres from north to south. The wall is very thick. The top is 2.8 metres. The exterior of the foundation has been partly destroyed, but it is still about 3 metres thick. The original wall is calculated to have been as thick as 5 metres. The wall is now 10.9 metres high with obvious narrowing at the top. It is built of rammed loess, each layer about 8 cm thick.

Layout and Structure of the Yumenguan Great Wall If you go out the west gate of Yumenguan and follow the interior part of the wall, the road will lead you straight to Lop Nur in Xinjiang — the Salt Marsh of ancient times.

The Great Wall here is not in very good condition, but the grandeur is still there. The highest section is about 300 metres to the east of Danggusui Beacon Tower. The present-day wall is 3.2 metres high and over 2 metres thick, built of sand, crushed stones, tamarisk branches or reeds. The process was first to choose a favourable site, then dig a not-too-deep foundation, put some reeds or tamarisk branches on it, follow with a layer of sand and stones, then another layer of reeds, and so on, until the wall reached several metres. Each reed layer should be 4 to 5 cm thick and each layer of sand and stones about 20 cm thick. From the remains of such walls one can see that some layers of sand and stones have become solid and some have even become part of the reed layers.

Beacon Towers at Yumenguan Standing on top of the Yumenguan fortification, one can see remains of many beacon towers inside and outside the wall.

Danggusui Beacon Tower is located about 4 kilometres west of Yumenguan, close to the inner side of the Great Wall. It is square with a high watchtower. Southeast of the watchtower are the remains of a few small rooms that supposedly were for the guards to live in when they were on duty. Stairs lead to the tower, so soldiers could climb the tower to watch and send signals. The tower's earthen platform is square, each side 7.8 metres long. The remains of the earthen platform are 7.8 metres high, with a distinct narrowing at the top. The structure and method of construction were the same as for the Great Wall — also reeds, sand and stones. On top of the watchtower some beams remain; perhaps they were where soldiers stood to watch or light the signals. The most distinguishing feature of the structure is the staircases that lead to the top. The corners of the stairs were the parts most easily destroyed. If reeds, sand and stones were used, they could never stand great pressure. Therefore, several dozen layers of fibres, about 10 centimetres thick, were stuck together. Even today some steps are in good condition.

Among the remains of beacon towers near the Great Wall and the fortifications at Yumenguan, many wooden slips, dating back to the Han Dynasty, were excavated in the late 18th century. On these slips is a record of Yumenguan, the Great Wall and the beacon towers at that time.

The district military commander's office under the jurisdiction of Dunhuang Prefecture was located at Yumenguan. Under him he had dozens of minor and major officers and 15 signal stations, which guarded that part of the wall.

The signal stations were distributed in three ways: along the wall, both inside and outside it; certain distances apart, forming a line without any wall (such as the section from outside Yumenguan to Puchanghai); connecting prefectural towns or other political and military centres. These last were few and far between. Remains of such signal stations between Yumenguan and Dunhuang exist today.

A signal station includes a watchtower for observing the enemy's movements and for sending signals. Under it are rooms for the soldiers to live in. Beside some of the watchtowers are horse sheds, sheep pens and storerooms for weapons and such. The watchtowers of the Han Dynasty were mostly square with an obvious narrowing at the top. They were about 12 metres high. Some were built of rammed earth, while others reeds, tamarisk branches, sand and stones, depending on available materials. The stations' four major tasks were to maintain the security of the signal station, watching for enemies and passing on informations; to safeguard villages and fields; to examine and protect traders and travelers; and to support the defence of nearby prefectures and counties.

The *Records of the Historian* and the *History of the Han Dynasty* contain detailed accounts of the building of Yumenguan and the Great Wall west of the Yellow River. By 111 B.C., during the reign of Wu Di of the Han Dynasty, the four prefectures — Wuwei, Zhangye, Jiuquan and Dunhuang — had been established. By 108 B.C. fortifications had been built from Jiuquan to Yumen; and by 101 B.C. from Yumen to the Salt Marsh. Construction of the Great Wall on the west bank of the Yellow River, over 2,000 li long, was completed within 10 years. The remains of the Yumenguan Great Wall and signal stations date back more than 2,000 years.

APPENDICES

Legends of the Great Wall

King You of Zhou Plays a Trick on His Dukes

Ruins of ancient beacon towers, first built in the Western Zhou Dynasty 3,000 years ago, can still be seen on top of Lishan Mountain in Lintong County, Shaanxi Province. At that time beacon fires were used to signal the alarm against external aggressors. They were very efficient.

King You of Zhou was enthroned in 781 B.C. At that time an earthquake occurred and natural disasters came one after another, so local communities asked for emergency help. In the west the strong Quanrong tribe threatened the safety of Zhou. Loyal ministers warned the King, but he turned a deaf ear to them, spent his days drinking wine and often sent people to find beauties for him. The honest ministers were exiled or imprisoned.

Minister Bao Xiang had been in prison for three years for trying to persuade the King. His son, Hong De, tried every means to rescue him, but in vain. Hong De decided he had to find a beauty for the King in order to ingratiate himself with him. One day he happened to meet a girl named Bao Si in the countryside. She looked just like a fairy, though she wore very ordinary clothes with no adornment. Hong De bought her

from her parents. After dressing her up, he presented her to King You. As soon as the King saw her, he loved her very much, so he ordered Bao Xiang released at once and restored to his original post.

After that King You did not take care of any official matters. He thought Bao Si was beyond compare, and he played and drank all day long with her. Everything seemed to be all right with Bao Si, but since she had come into the palace she had never laughed. In order to make Bao Si laugh the King gathered many musicians and dancers to sing and dance. All to no avail. Then he issued a proclamation. Anyone who could make Bao Si laugh would be awarded 1,000 *liang* of gold.

Treacherous court officials busied themselves with making suggestions. One minister, named Guo Shifu, went to the King and said with narrowed eyes, "There are twenty beacon towers on Lishan Mountain east of the capital that our predecessors built in order to guard against Quanrong invaders. Fires were burnt to ask for help from dukes when enemies came. But now we have a peaceful life and the beacon towers haven't been used for a long time. How would it be if Your Majesty and Lady Bao went there to burn fires? Dukes would come quickly with their soldiers. When Lady Bao saw so many soldiers and horses rushing to and fro for nothing, she would have to laugh. I am sure of it." The King agreed with the minister at once.

As soon as Minister Zheng Boyou, the King's uncle, heard of the plan, he rushed to Lishan Mountain and said to the King, "You can't do that! These beacon towers were built by our forefathers. If our country should really be in danger afterwards, no one would come to the rescue!"

When the King heard that, he was very angry. He said, "Now everything is peaceful. The beacon towers are no use at all. We came here just for fun. If something happens afterwards, that has nothing to do with you!"

Night fell. The King ordered fires burned and in the twinkling of an eye flames towered to the sky. Then he ordered drums beaten to urge his soldiers. As soon as the dukes saw beacon fires they thought the capital was in danger, so they led troops to the capital. When they arrived, there was nothing happening there. The people told them the King was on Lishan Mountain, so they turned east to run several dozen li to Lishan. They were very tired, but what did they see! The King and Bao Si were drinking while watching the fire. There were no invaders. The officers and soldiers got very angry, but they just stood there, not knowing what to do. Then the King gave an order: "There are no invaders; you can go back now." The dukes looked at each other, not knowing whether to laugh or cry. They had to go back. When Bao Si saw the scene, she could not help laughing. The King was pleased and said, "Ah! You are so pretty when you laugh. The credit should go to Guo Shifu." The King granted Guo Shifu a lot of money at once.

Not long after, Quanrong invaders attacked the capital. The capital was really in danger. The King lighted the beacon fires again, but no one came because they did not want to be fooled again. The capital quickly fell into the enemy's hands. King You and Bao Si ran to Lishan Mountain. The invaders followed close upon them, killed the King and took Bao Si away. The 300-year-old Western Zhou Dynasty was destroyed during the reign of King You.

Retold by Wen Yuan

— 45 —

Meng Jiangnü Looks for Her Husband

It is said that a section of the Great Wall had to be rebuilt after Meng Jiangnü's tears made it collapse.

Long, long ago there were two families who lived side by side near Badaling. Both the families had no children; for many years they had got along very well together.

One year the Meng family planted a melon seed that grew and grew. The vine climbed the wall to the other side and a melon appeared. The melon grew bigger and bigger day by day. People enjoyed watching it. In the autumn it was ripe. The melon belonged to both families, so it had to be cut in half.

After drying in the sun for three days, it was cut. Eh? No pulp, no seeds, but a pretty little girl with two big eyes sat inside. The two families were astonished. They hired a wet nurse for her.

In a flash the girl was a dozen years old. The two families were rich, especially the Meng family, so they got a tutor for her. She was given the name Meng Jiangnü (the Girl of the Mengs and Jiangs) because she was a child of both the Meng and the Jiang family.

At that time Emperor Qin Shi Huang was building the Great Wall. It was a big project so it needed a lot of people. Young men were pressganged into building the Great Wall. There was no set time for their return.

A young scholar named Fan Xiliang [known as Fan Qiliang in another version of the tale] was afraid of being pressganged, so he ran away from his home. He didn't know where to go, but he decided to find a place with no sign of human habitation. After a while he saw nothing around him and stopped. He was afraid he would die of hunger in that place. Then he struggled on. Soon he glimpsed a village in the distance. He was so pleased he ran there. Entering the village, he saw a garden. Quickly he ran into the garden to hide himself.

It was the Meng family's garden. Meng Jiangnü was there. When she saw a man under the grapevine trellis, she was frightened and cried for help, "There is a man here! There is a man here!"

The servant girl with her also saw the man and cried too. Fan Xiliang hurried out and said, "Don't cry! Don't cry! Please help me! I am running for my life."

Meng Jiangnü looked the young man up and down. He was just like a scholar and not a bad person, so she went to her father and told him about the young man. Her father let the young man come into his room.

Fan Xiliang was trembling and his head bowed low when he entered the room. Meng Jiangnü's father asked him, "Where did you come from, and why did you run away from home?"

Fan Xiliang was allowed to stay in the Meng home because of his honesty.

Several days later he and Meng Jiangnü began studying together.

One day Meng Jiangnü's father said to his wife, "Fan Xiliang is a very good young man. How about letting our daughter marry him?"

The old woman was pleased, but she said that they should not hurry and should first consult the Jiang family.

The old man and woman of the Jiang family were pleased with the idea, so the matter was settled.

The families picked an auspicious day for the wedding and invited all their friends and relatives to eat and drink all day long.

The man servant in Meng's home had wanted to marry Meng Jiangnü for a long time. He thought it was Fan Xiliang who had made his dream vanish like soap bubbles. He decided not to let the couple lead a happy life and reported to the county magistrate that the Meng family had sheltered a labourer on the Great Wall and his name was Fan Xiliang.

As soon as the magistrate heard that, he led some yamen runners to Meng's family.

It was getting dark and all the guests had left for home. When the bride and bridegroom were getting ready to go into the bridal chamber, they heard a great noise. The runners rushed into the bridal chamber and seized Fan Xiliang. He was not even allowed to say farewell.

Meng Jiangnü's face turned deathly pale with anger and she stamped her foot in fury. She cried for a while, but there was nothing she could do. Several days later she told her parents she would go to the construction site to find her husband.

Since they could do nothing to comfort her, they gave her some silver and sent the man servant to accompany her.

Halfway there the servant began to take liberties with Meng Jiangnü. He said to her, "Is it worth your going such a long distance to look for Fan Xiliang? I am sure he is already dead. What would you think of living with me?"

As soon as she heard that, she knew clearly he was going to play a dirty trick, but she was afraid of offending him because she could not find anyone to help her in that place. So she pretended to agree with him and said, "All right, but we have to find a matchmaker."

That put him on the spot. He had no idea what to do.

Then Meng Jiangnü pointed to the valley and said, "I have an idea. You see that flower over there? You go fetch it and it will be the matchmaker."

The servant was very glad and said the flower was easy to get, but when he saw the steep precipice, he was frightened. Meng Jiangnü said, "You are a man and you should have courage. Here is a rope on this package. How about my lowering you with this rope?"

He thought that was a good idea, so Meng Jiangnü held one end of the rope and the servant held the other. Half down she let the rope go. Then she heard his scream and the thud of his landing. She was very pleased he had fallen to his death. He was just like a toad lusting after swan's flesh. He had got just what he deserved.

After that she packed up her things and went to the construction site of the Great Wall. She saw huge crowds of people there. She asked for Fan Xiliang, but nobody knew him. Then she saw some people taking a break. She went towards them and asked, "Is Fan Xiliang here?" They answered, "He was here several days ago, but we have not seen him since. Perhaps he is dead." Meng Jiangnü was surprised to hear this and asked hurriedly, "Where did he die and where is his corpse?"

The man sighed. "Who takes care of the corpses of labourers! When a labourer is dead, his corpse is carried away to fill the foot of the Great Wall."

She was very grieved and cried till dark. Just then a section of the Great Wall crashed down and Fan Xiliang's corpse fell out. She rushed there and cried, holding her husband's corpse close. Not long after, a group of soldiers kidnapped her and took

her to the county magistrate. When the magistrate saw how beautiful Meng Jiangnü was, he got an evil idea. He presented her to Qin Shi Huang.

Qin Shi Huang rewarded the county magistrate with gold, silver and other treasures and also promoted him. Qin Shi Huang wanted to take Meng Jiangnü as his own, but she refused him. The Emperor asked several old women to try to persuade her, but it was in vain. Meng Jiangnü stayed there quite a long time and finally decided it was not the way to solve the problem. After thinking it over, she said to the old women, "I agree with the Emperor." The women reported to Qin Shi Huang, and he immediately went to Meng Jiangnü with great pleasure. When Meng Jiangnü saw him, she said he had to agree to do three things. The Emperor thought, "So long as she is willing, I shall do thirty things for her, not just three."

"First," Meng Jiangnü said, "you must invite eminent monks and Taoist priests to pray for my late husband for forty-nine days in a beautifully decorated shed." After thinking it over, Qin Shi Huang agreed.

Then Meng Jiangnü said, "Second, you must put on mourning dress and kneel before the bier and call 'Father' three times."

Qin Shi Huang hesitated. He was an emperor; how could he do such a thing? Finally he said he couldn't do that and asked what the third thing was.

"If you can't do the second thing, I won't tell you the third," Meng Jiangnü said.

Qin Shi Huang thought it over again, and again he couldn't make up his mind. But he didn't want to pass up such a good opportunity, because Meng Jiangnü was too pretty. At last he agreed to the second request.

"Third, you have to go boating with me for three days. After that we will get married," the girl said.

The Emperor did not hesitate to agree to the last request. Then he ordered that eminent monks and Taoist priests be invited, and he put up a shed. When the monks and priests were chanting scriptures, the Emperor put on mourning dress.

After that Meng Jiangnü asked the Emperor to get ready to go to sea. Qin Shi Huang was overjoyed and ordered his servants to prepare two sedan chairs and two pleasure boats. They went to the seashore in the sedan chairs. When they arrived there, Meng Jiangnü got directly into the boat. When they rowed to the middle of the sea, she jumped into the water.

That threw the Emperor into a panic. He shouted for help, but before people could come, she had already sunk to the bottom. Now he knew he had been tricked by the girl. He was very angry and took out his mountain-moving whip, which he had seized from a priest. He wanted to press Meng

Jiangnü to the bottom of the sea by casting rocks into it with the magic whip.

But the Dragon King of the sea wouldn't tolerate it. He was worried over what would happen to his Dragon Palace if the sea were full of rocks.

He had a princess who was very smart. She said to her father, "Don't worry! I am going to get the whip."

"How can you get it?"

"I am going to change into Meng Jiangnü and marry the Emperor so I can get it."

After the Dragon King heard that, he was overjoyed. "It's a good idea. You can go at once."

When the Dragon Princess came out of the water, she saw the Emperor was still whipping at rocks, and said to him, "I told you before we would play at sea for three days. It is now only about two days and you are whipping at rocks to fill the sea. It is lucky I have not been hurt."

As soon as the Emperor saw Meng Jiangnü, he put his whip back and said, "I thought you would not come back." Then they went home. The Dragon Princess stayed with the Emperor for 100 days, then she went away, taking the whip with her.

Retold by Zhang Zicheng

Song of Meng Jiangnü

Plum blossoms for the lunar New Year,
Every family lights a red lamp.
Husbands of all the other families come back
*   home,*
But Meng Jiangnü's husband is building the
*   Great Wall.*

When the apricot is blossoming,
The weather is warm.
Swallows fly to the south in pairs,
And in pairs they build their nests neatly
On the beams of the house.

When the peach tree is in blossom,
Qingming Festival is coming.
Every family is busy getting ready to visit
*   graves to honour the dead,*
Red tears flow from the peach blossom in
*   rain,*
Meng Jiangnü's home is cheerless.

When the herbaceous peony is in blossom,
People begin to raise silkworms.
Meng Jiangnü, a basket on her arm, is going
*   to pick mulberry leaves,*
She hangs the basket on a branch of the tree.
While she is picking the leaves,
Tears roll down her cheeks.

When the pomegranate is as red as the plum,
Meng Jiangnü thinks of her husband and her
*   eyes are full of tears.*
Seedlings in the fields are green,
But Meng Jiangnü's land is overgrown with
*   weeds.*

Lotus is in blossom,
And the weather is terribly hot.
Mosquitoes fly to Meng Jiangnü and bite her,
She would rather the insects bite her a thou-
*   sand times*
Than bite her husband.

When garden balsam is in blossom,
A cool autumn breeze blows.
Every family is busy sewing clothes,
The husbands of the other families have
*   changed their clothes,*
But Meng Jiangnü's husband still has no
*   padded jacket.*

Sweet osmanthus is in full bloom,
A solitary wild goose flies with frost on its
*   head.*
Just like the solitary wild goose
A pair of mandarin ducks is separated.

When the chrysanthemum blooms,
The Double Ninth Festival is coming.

Good wine with chrysanthemum fragrance is
  prepared for the festival,
She is in no mood to drink wine without her
  husband,
Keep the wine until she can toast her husband.

The cottonrose hibiscus is flowering,
But Meng Jiangnü is home feeling miserable.
Husbands of the other families have changed
  into their cotton-padded clothes,
But Meng Jiangnü's husband hasn't changed
  his colothes yet.

Snowflakes are flying,
Meng Jiangnü has gone a thousand li carrying

winter clothing.
She has cried down a hundred thousand li of
  Great Wall
And sadly recognized her husband's bones.

Fragrant narcissus is blossoming,
Jiangnü's parents miss her greatly.
Last New Year's Eve the three of them kept
  watch,
But this year Jiangnü is in the sea.

Collated by Zhang Zicheng

A Tale of Xifengkou

There are many famous gateways along the Great Wall. Xifengkou, near the Luanhe River north of Qian'an County, Hebei Province, is one of them.

It used to be called Songtingguan in ancient times. Mountains lined both sides of the pass and a river flowed through it, so it was difficult of access. Ancient books say that carts could pass through Shanhaiguan and Juyongguan, but only a single person could walk through Xifengkou. The mountains north of the pass were especially precipitous. Xifengkou was not easy to attack because of its strong gatetower, moat and wall, and the pass was guarded all year long.

A young man named Wang Bao'er was good at farm work. When he was 22 years old, he was enlisted as a guardian of the pass. Because he was young and clever, he was kept there while others returned home upon termination of their service.

Wang Bao'er's father was an old peasant. Every day he expected his son to come home, for the latter's absence had increased his burden. He got up early and went to bed late every day. He missed his son very much. He recalled that when his son was little, he had given him the best care, but now it had been 20 years since he had seen him. He couldn't bear it any longer. He wanted to look for his son, but he worried about the long journey. After thinking it over and over, he made up his mind. He decided if he did not go to see his son, he might not see him again, because he was so old.

He went directly north with a bundle under his arm. At night he slept in sheds, and when he was hungry, he picked hazelnuts and wild fruits.

He asked people along the way, "Where is the pass of the Great Wall?" People told him the direction to go in. Day after day he got nearer the Great Wall. One day he came to a river between two steep mountains. After crossing the river, he felt very hungry. On a tree near a cave he saw a bird's nest in which there were many eggs. He took some eggs and cooked them over pine branches. After that he continued his journey. Before long he saw the gatetower of the pass of the Great Wall. He was very happy at the thought he would soon see his son.

When he was near the pass, he saw several soldiers carrying wood, so he went up to them and asked, "Do you know Wang Bao'er?" "Yes," they said, "he went to the mountains to cut trees thirty li away. He'll come back at sunset."

He had found his son at last! He waited several hours until dark, then he saw several soldiers coming down from a mountain shouldering wood. By that time Wang Bao'er was nearly 40 years old. When he heard someone calling him, he ran as fast as he could. He saw an old man with white hair. He could not even recognize his father at first.

They were so happy they wept and laughed at the same time in each other's arms. The old man said, "My son, I have found you at last!   Heaven has given my son back to me!"

As he spoke his hands began to shake. The shaking would not stop, until finally he died.   Extreme joy had begot sorrow.

The son was very sad at his father's death and cried every day.   Several days later he died also.   Father and son were buried at the roadside and in their honour the pass was named Xifengkou (Joy Meeting Gateway).   Later the name was changed to Joy Peak Gateway.

Retold by Zhao Luo

The Shoulder Pole of the God Erlang

An interesting story is told in Xinglong and Zunhua counties of Hebei Province. It seems there was a village named Huangmenzi between the two counties, surrounded by steep, yellow cliffs, with green pines on the mountaintop and clear streams at its foot. Since ancient times no one had been able to climb to the top of the mountain, but strangely enough, a pole three metres long was stuck halfway up. Looking up, people could see the pole clearly. They asked, "How did the pole get there if no one has climbed up?"

It is said there were nine suns in ancient times. When one sun set, another rose, so there was daylight all year round. All living things dried up. People had a hard time living. Just at that time the emperor Qin Shi Huang enlisted hundreds of thousands of labourers to build the Great Wall. They were tired out from shouldering stones and earth under the scorching sun. Some got seriously sick and some died. Those who could not continue working were thrown into the Great Wall as filler.

This event disturbed the god Erlang in Heaven. When he looked down from the clouds, he saw a dense crowd at the foot of the mountains shouldering stones and earth. When he looked up, he saw nine suns rising in turn. He knew clearly the people could no longer work so hard under the sun. If things went on like that, people would die of fatigue and the heat. So he changed himself into an old man with a white beard and went to the overseer and said,

"You should do some good things for these people. You see, they are panting from the heat of the nine suns and the heavy work, and you often beat them with whips and wooden sticks. They will die of the hardship. You should let them have a break and drink some water."

The overseer said impatiently, "Who will build the Great Wall if they have a rest? Go away quickly, or I'll beat you to death!"

The god Erlang said angrily, "You let them have a rest and some water! I'll do as much as they would!"

The overseer replied fiercely, "Look at yourself! You would fall down at a gust of wind. How can you do the work for them? You're looking for trouble! If you can't carry the stones and finish the work in time, I'll bury you under the Great Wall, so you can never rise up again."

As soon as the overseer had spoken, Erlang jumped onto a big stone and shouted, stroking his beard, "Hey! All of you! Take a rest and drink some water!"

When the men heard the shouting, they stopped working and lay down on the ground. Soon they were sound asleep.

Shouldering two mountains on a pole, the god started driving away the suns. As soon as a sun rose, he struck it with a mountain. He had knocked down eight suns when his shoulder pole broke. A mountain fell out of his basket and killed the overseer. The workers woke with a start at the noise of the breaking of the shoulder pole. They saw the old man pulling the shoulder pole from the mountain. Some workers cried in alarm, "Get up quickly! The suns have been knocked down by an old man!"

As soon as the old man heard the shouting, he put down the broken pole and disappeared in a gust of wind.

That is why there is a shoulder pole in the middle of Huangmenzi Mountain, and the sun we see now is the one the god Erlang left. From that time on there has been day and night in the world.

Retold by Cheng Yun

A Brick from Jiayuguan

A builder, Yi Kaizhan, was asked to build Jiayuguan, the pass at the west end of the Great Wall. He was good at arithmetic and could calculate accurately how much material and how many days a project would need. He had done that kind of work before on several projects.

A supervisor, Zhang Buxin, who was responsible for the project, did not believe in Yi's ability. Yi Kaizhan bet that the number of bricks would be accurate. Zhang Buxin said, "You had better add one more brick in case it is not enough. If it is left over, I will put it on Chongguan Gatetower in your name. Is that all right?"

"That's settled!" Yi Kaizhan replied readily.

Yi Kaizhan won the bet. There was just one brick left after finishing the pass. This brick is still on top of Chongguan Gatetower today.

Retold by Tang Guangyu

The Swallow Cries at Jiayuguan

If you throw a stone at the north corner of the east and west gatetowers of Jiayuguan and to the left and right outside the castle gate, you can hear a sweet sound just like a swallow's cry. This is well known at Jiayuguan.

Jiayuguan was a heavily guarded pass at the west end of the Ming Dynasty Great Wall. Its gate opened and closed at fixed times. When the gate was closed, nobody could enter the pass, not even birds and beasts.

It is said that a pair of swallows lived inside Jiayuguan. Every morning they flew out of the pass and returned before the closing of the gate. One day the two swallows flew away together in the morning, but only one of them came back before closing time. The other one was late because she had flown too far to come back on time. When she arrived at the gate, she entreated the guard to let her in, but the guard said, "I am responsible for the safety of the pass. If I break the regulation, I will be punished. Without an order from higher authority I won't let anybody in, not even the emperor."

Hearing that, the swallow knew there was no way out, so she threw herself hard against the wall and fell to the ground. She let out one sad cry, then died. It is said the sound people can hear now in this place is the spirit of the swallow.

In fact, the spot is just a 90-degree angle, and the wall is strong, made of fine-quality bricks. So the echo of a hard cobblestone thrown against the wall can be heard clearly.

Retold by Luo Zhewen

A general.

Qin buried sculptures of troops and horses. In 221 B.C. Qin Shi Huang conquered six states and founded the first unified nation in China's history. After he died, a large number of life-size pottery troops and horses were arranged in battle formation and buried beside Qin Shi Huang's tomb as his guard. These terra-cotta figures, as well as a bronze chariot and horses, have been unearthed in Lintong County, Shaanxi Province. They are now on display in the Museum of Qin Shi Huang's Buried Sculptures.

Infantrymen in battle array.

The newly unearthed bronze chariot and horses.

Terra-cotta troops and horses in battle array.

Han Dynasty troops and horses.

Ming Dynasty stone carvings of palace guards.

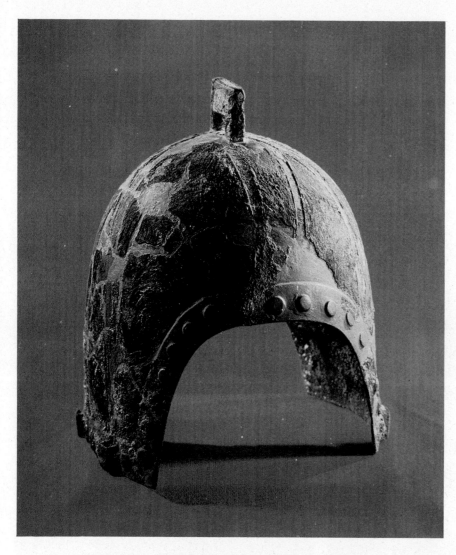

Bronze helmet.

Sword used by Gou Jian, king of Yue, more than 2,000 years ago.

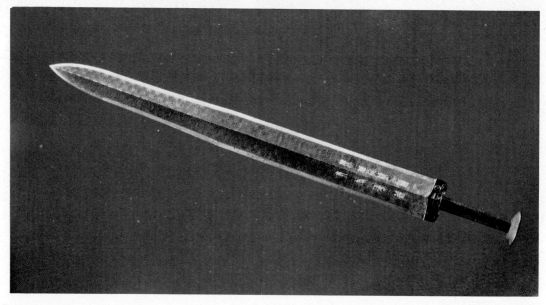

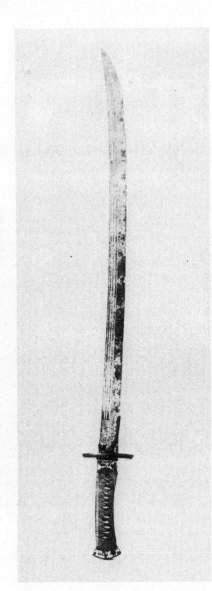

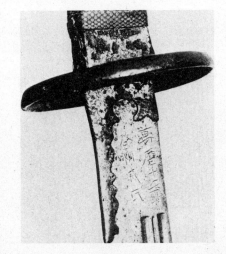

Dagger (with detail) used by General Qi Jiguang.

A caltrop.

An iron spearhead.

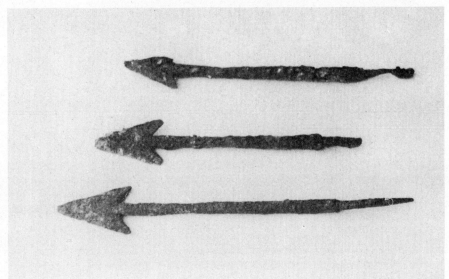

Three iron arrowheads.

Ming Dynasty iron cannon, now on display on the Shanhaiguan wall.

Gunpowder found on Jinshanling Great Wall in Luanping County, Hebei Province.

Small cannonballs
(dia. 20 to 30 mm).

Big cannonballs
(dia. 60 to 80 mm).

Grenades.

A *lingpai* (order conferred by a high officer as a token of authority).

A *yaopai* (a pass the holder wears at his waist).

A Han Dynasty bronze statue of chariot and officer.

Han Dynasty bronze statues of cavalrymen.

Pottery cavalryman.

Chronological Table of Chinese History

Xia		Around 21st to 16th century B.C.
Shang		Around 16th to 11th century B.C.
Western Zhou		Around 11th century to 770 B.C.
Eastern Zhou	Spring and Autumn Period	770—476 B.C.
	Warring States Period	475—221 B.C.
Qin		221—207 B.C.
Western Han		206 B.C.—A.D. 25
Eastern Han		25—220
Three Kingdoms (Wei, Shu, Wu)		220—265
Western Jin		265—316
Eastern Jin		317—420
Southern and Northern Dynasties		420—589
Sui		581—618
Tang		618—907
Five Dynasties		907—960
Song (Northern and Southern)		960—1279
Liao		916—1125
Western Xia		1038—1227
Kin		1115—1234
Yuan		1271—1368
Ming		1368—1644
Qing		1644—1911

Genealogical Table of the Qin, Han and Ming Dynasties

In these three dynasties a tremendous amount of work was done on the Great Wall.

Qin (221-207 B.C.)

Royal Titles	Names	Period of Reign
First Emperor (Qin Shi Huang)	Ying Zheng	221—210 B.C.
Second Emperor	Hu Hai	209—207 B.C.

Western Han (206 B.C.-A.D. 25)

Royal Titles	Names	Period of Reign
Gao Di	Liu Bang	206—195 B.C.
Hui Di	Liu Ying	194—188 B.C.
Gao Hou	Lü Zhi	187—180 B.C.
Wen Di	Liu Heng	179—157 B.C.
Jing Di	Liu Qi	156—141 B.C.
Wu Di	Liu Che	140—87 B.C.
Zhao Di	Liu Fuling	86—74 B.C.
Xuan Di	Liu Xun	73—49 B.C.
Yuan Di	Liu Shi	48—33 B.C.
Cheng Di	Liu Ao	32—7 B.C.
Ai Di	Liu Xin	6—1 B.C.
Ping Di	Liu Kan	A.D. 1—5
Ru Zi Ying (with Wang Mang as regent)		6—8
(Xin) Wang Mang		9—22
Gengshi Di	Liu Xuan	23—25

Ming (1368-1644)

Royal Titles	Names	Period of Reign
Tai Zu	Zhu Yuanzhang	1368—1398
Hui Di	Zhu Yunwen	1399—1402
Cheng Zu	Zhu Di	1403—1424
Ren Zong	Zhu Gaozhi	1425
Xuan Zong	Zhu Zhanji	1426—1435
Ying Zong	Zhu Qizhen	1436—1449
Dai Zong	Zhu Qiyu	1450—1456
Ying Zong	Zhu Qizhen	1457—1464
Xian Zong	Zhu Jianshen	1465—1487
Xiao Zong	Zhu Youtang	1488—1505
Wu Zong	Zhu Houzhao	1506—1521
Shi Zong	Zhu Houzong	1522—1566
Mu Zong	Zhu Zaihou	1567—1572
Shen Zong	Zhu Yijun	1573—1620
Guang Zong	Zhu Changluo	1620
Xi Zong	Zhu Youjiao	1621—1627
Si Zong	Zhu Youjian	1628—1644

Units of Measure of Each Dynasty

Ancient China used the decimal system in measurement. One *zhang* is equal to 10 *chi;* 1 *chi* is equal to 10 *cun*; 1 *cun* is equal to 10 *fen*. One li is equal to 1,800 *chi*.

Dynasty or Period		One *chi* Converted to Metric System
Shang		0.169 m
Warring States Period		0.227 — 0.231 m
Western Han		0.230 m
Xin (Wang Mang)		0.231 m
Eastern Han		0.235 — 0.239 m
Three Kingdoms (Wei)		0.241 — 0.242 m
Jin		0.245 m
Song	Southern Dynasties	0.245 — 0.247 m
Liang		0.236 — 0.251 m
Northern Wei		0.255 — 0.295 m
Eastern Wei	Northern Dynasties	0.300 m
Northern Zhou		0.267 m
Sui		0.273 m
Tang		0.280 — 0.313 m
Song		0.309 — 0.329 m
Ming		0.320 m
Qing (before A.D. 1840)		0.310 — 0.320 m

Bibliography of Books on the Great Wall

1. *Zuo Zhuan* (*Zuo Qiuming's Commentary on the Spring and Autumn Annals*).
2. *Shi Ji* (*Records of the Historian*) by Sima Qian (c. 145 or 135 B.C.-?), Zhonghua Press, 1975.
3. *Han Shu* (*History of the Han Dynasty*) by Ban Gu (A.D. 32-92), Zhonghua Press, 1962.
4. *Shui Jing Zhu* (*Commentary on the "Waterways Classic"*) by Li Daoyuan (466 or 472-527), Ancient Book Publishing House, 1955.
5. *Zhu Shu Ji Nian* (*The Bamboo Annals*), an ancient chronological history book written on bamboo slips, published by New Knowledge Publishing House, 1956.
6. *Kuo Di Zhi Ji Xiao* (*Geographical Records*), a geography book of the Tang Dynasty, published by Zhonghua Press, 1980.
7. *Tong Dian* (*A Comprehensive Study of History*) by Du You (735-812), Commercial Press, 1935.
8. *Sui Shu* (*History of the Sui Dynasty*) by Wei Zheng (580-643) and others, Zhonghua Press, 1973.
9. *Bei Shi* (*History of the Northern Dynasties*) by Li Yanshou, Zhonghua Press, 1974.
10. *Zi Zhi Tong Jian* (*History as a Mirror*) by Sima Guang (1019-1086), Zhonghua Press, 1966.
11. *Wu Jing Zong Yao* (*Collection of the Most Important Military Techniques*), a military primer of the Northern Song Dynasty, published by Zhonghua Press, 1959.
12. *Ming Shi* (*History of the Ming Dynasty*) by Zhang Tingyu (1672-1755), Zhonghua Press, 1974.
13. *Huai Nan Zi* (*The Book of the Prince of Huainan*) by Liu An (179-122 B.C.) and others, Commercial Press, 1919.
14. *Wei Shu* (*History of the Wei Dynasty*) by Wei Shou, Zhonghua Press, 1974.
15. *Zhou Shu* (*History of the Zhou Dynasty*) by Linghu Defen and others, Zhonghua Press, 1974.
16. *The Great Wall*, a pictorial album, compiled by Yu Jin, Historical Relics Publishing House, 1980.

中国的万里长城

罗哲文　赵洛　著

*

外文出版社出版
（中国北京百万庄路24号）
外文印刷厂印刷
中国国际图书贸易总公司
（中国国际书店）发行
北京399信箱
1986年（16开）第一版
编号：（英）12050—69
01430
12—E—1874P